ENGLISH G

LIGHTHOUSE | HEADLIGHT | HIGHLIGHT

Workbook
Förderausgabe

AUDIOS online

1

Deine Audios findest du hier:

1. Melde dich auf scook.de an.
2. Gib den unten stehenden Zugangscode in die Box ein.
3. Hab viel Spaß mit den Audios.

Dein Zugangscode auf www.scook.de

Die Audios können dort nach Bestätigung der AGB und Lizenzbedingungen genutzt werden.

ouun2-dont5

Cornelsen

INHALT

In deinem Arbeitsheft gibt es viele Zeichen vor den Aufgaben. Sie helfen dir, die Arbeitsanweisungen zu verstehen und geben Hinweise auf Hilfsmittel, die du benötigst. Das bedeuten sie:

	Höre dir den genannten CD-Track an.
	Lies genau.
	Nimm dir einen Stift.
	Du musst (mit jemandem) sprechen.
	Sieh dir die Bilder genau an.
	Hake die richtige Lösung ab.
	Suche dir eine Partnerin / einen Partner.
grün	Ersetze die grünen Wörter mit eigenen Ideen.
orange	Wähle zwischen den orangen Wörtern aus.
blau	Blau zeigt dir ein Beispiel.

Nice to meet you![1]

1 Read and write.

eleven • ~~Julian~~ • from • in Germany

2 a) Read and write.

~~Tim~~ •
eleven •
Plymouth

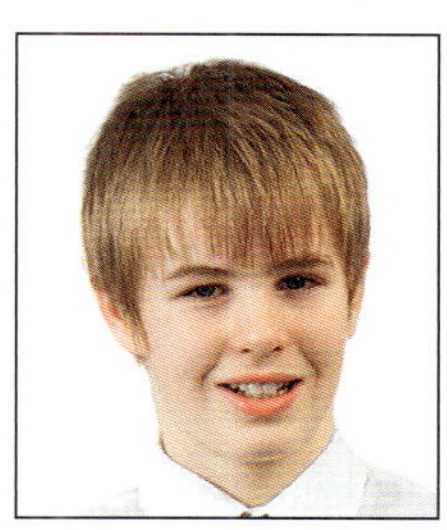

Holly •
ten •
London

Hi. I'm Tim.
What's your name?

I'm eleven.
What about you?

I'm from Plymouth.
What about you?

I'm Holly.
Nice to meet you.

I'm ten.

I'm from
London.

b) Act the dialogue with a partner.

1 in EG HL: Hi! What's your name?

3 a) Colour the pairs[1].

four
six
one
ten
seven
twelve

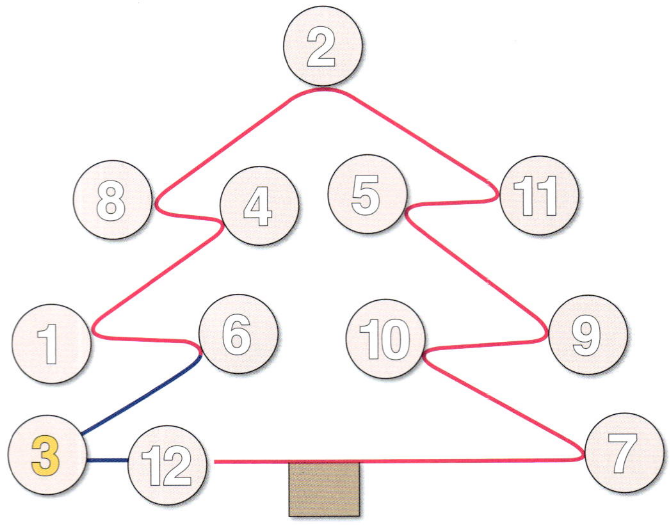

eight
two
eleven
five
three
nine

b) Listen and join[2] the numbers.

1

4 a) Listen and write.

2

What's your phone number, Kate?

2 7 1 3 9 5

b) What's your and your partner's phone number? Ask and write.

Lösungs-beispiel

– My number: 4 5 8 9 7 1

– David 's number: 3 8 1 2 6 4

5 Find the numbers and circle.

one

three

two

g	p	m	t	w	o
m	a	w	h	u	s
f	o	u	r	z	i
r	k	s	e	t	x
d	o	n	e	x	h
h	c	f	i	v	e

four

six

five

1 pair: *Paar* 2 join: *verbinden*

► SB LH/HD/HL, pp. 8–9

6 Listen and colour.

Kevin	Polly	Fred	Jack	Lisa	Rick	Lucy
(yellow)	(blue)	(black)	(red)	(green)	(white)	(brown)

7 Look and write.

yellow • orange • black • pink • ~~blue~~ • green

1

I like blue sweets.

I don't like yellow sweets.

2

I like orange sweets.

I don't like black sweets.

3

I like green sweets.

I don't like pink sweets.

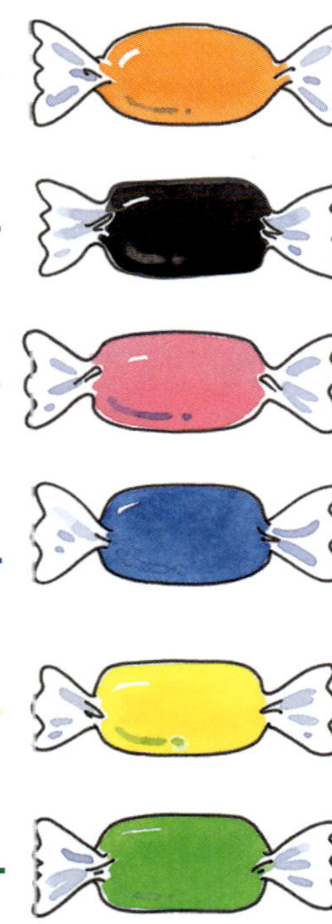

8 Colour the German[1] and the British flag[2].

1 = white
2 = yellow
3 = red
4 = blue
5 = black

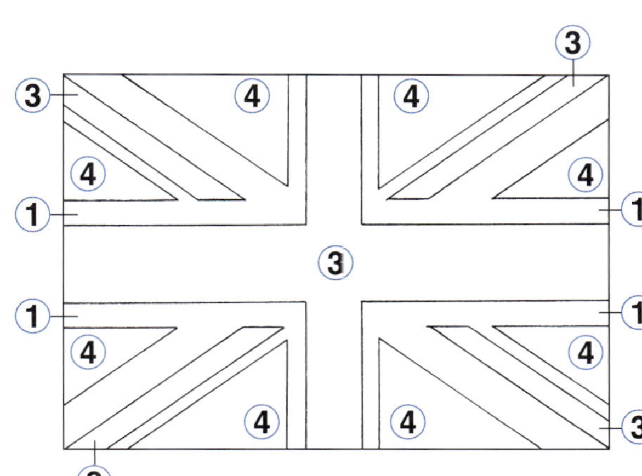

1 German: *deutsch* 2 flag: *Flagge*

► *SB LH/HD/HL, p. 10*

9 Look and write.

a bird • two birds • a cat (2x) • an elephant • and three dogs • I have (3x)

10 a) Look, read and say.

b) Write the sentences.

1 

2 

3 

4 

The cat | is | black.

is

The dog

old.

The bird

small.

is

The elephant

is

big.

1 The cat is black.

2 The dog is old.

3 The bird is small.

4 The elephant is big.

► SB LH/HD/HL, p. 12

11 a) Look and write.

dancing • reading • football • watching TV • ~~swimming~~ • I like • I don't like

1 

I like swimming and dancing.

2 

I don't like watching TV.

3 

I like reading.

4 

I don't like football and watching TV.

A 

B 

C 

D 

E 

b) What do you like? What don't you like? Write. Then tell a partner.

Lösungs-beispiel

☺ I like football.

☹ I don't like dancing.

12 Look and write.

bike • ~~I'm~~ • like • mobile • new • playing games • red • small • Tom

Hi, I'm Sarah.
My favourite thing is my bike.
It's new.
I like my bike. It's great.

Hi, I'm Tom.
My favourite thing is my mobile.
It's red and it's small.
I like playing games on it.

► SB LH/HD/HL, pp. 11–13

13 Write the words.

~~big~~ • Germany • new • old • small • white

i g b	1 big	w e n	4 new
l d o	2 old	l s l a m	5 small
i h t e w	3 white	e G r y a n m	6 Germany

14 a) Read Luca's email.

Diese E-Mail kannst du als Muster für deine eigene E-Mail in **14 b** verwenden. Ersetze einfach die grünen Wörter durch deine eigenen Ideen.

Subject: Hello from Luca

Hello! I'm Luca.
I'm from Plymouth in England.
I'm ten. I like swimming.
My favourite colour is black.
My favourite animal is a cat.
My favourite thing is my bike.
What about you?
Goodbye!
Luca

b) Now you. Write an email.

Lösungsbeispiel

Subject: Re: Hello from Luca

Hello! I'm Nina.
I'm from Dortmund in Germany.
I'm eleven.
I like reading.
My favourite colour is blue.
My favourite animal is a dog.
My favourite thing is my bike.
Goodbye!
Nina

eleven • twelve • ...

reading • football • ...

blue • green • red • ...

a bird • a cat • a dog • ...

bike • computer • mobile • ...

▸ SB LH/HD/HL, pp. 13–14

Welcome to our school

1 Look and write.

bike • boy • car • ~~girl~~ • mobile phone • teacher

1 a girl

2 a car

3 a teacher

4 a boy

5 a bike

6 a mobile phone

2 a) Listen and write.

4

Bye! • I'm OK, thanks. • I'm from Hannover. • ~~Hello!~~ • I'm eleven. • I'm Olivia.

1

2

3

4

5

6

b) Act the dialogues with a partner.

▸ SB LH / HD / HL, pp. 16–17

3 a) Look and write.

1

I have two brothers.

- I have no brothers and sisters.
- I have one brother.
- I have one sister.
- I have two brothers.

2

I have one sister.

3

I have one brother.

4
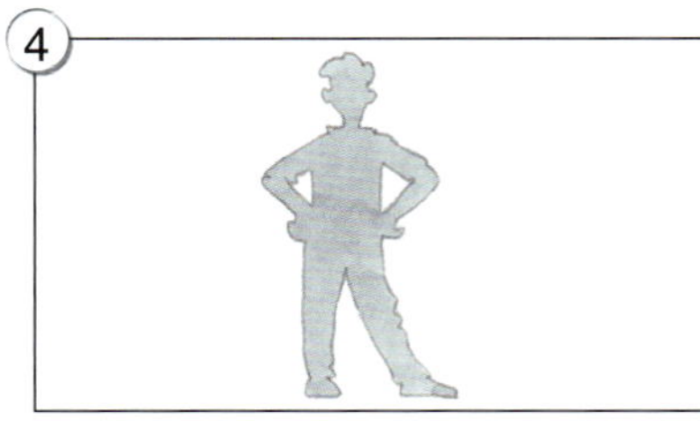

I have no brothers and sisters.

b) Look and write.

two brothers • I have • three sisters • and (2x) • two sisters • a dog

1

I have two brothers and two sisters.

2

I have three sisters and a dog.

4 Listen and circle.

5

1 Hello, Mrs Lee. I'm Catherine / Holly.

2 I'm eleven / twelve.

3 I have two / three sisters.

4 I have no / two brothers.

5 My cat is big / small and white and my fish is small and orange / white.

6 I like reading and I like riding / dancing too.

7 My favourite sport is football / swimming.

► SB LH / HD / HL, pp. 18–19

5 a) **Listen and tick.**

school: *Eggbuckland Community College*	class: *6K*	name: *Jack*			
lesson	Monday	Tuesday	Wednesday	Thursday	Friday
maths	✓	✓	☐	☐	✓
history	☐	☐	☐	✓	✓
science	✓	✓	☐	☐	☐
art	☐	☐	✓	☐	☐
English	✓	☐	☐	✓	☐
German	☐	✓	✓	☐	☐

b) **Write your timetable.**

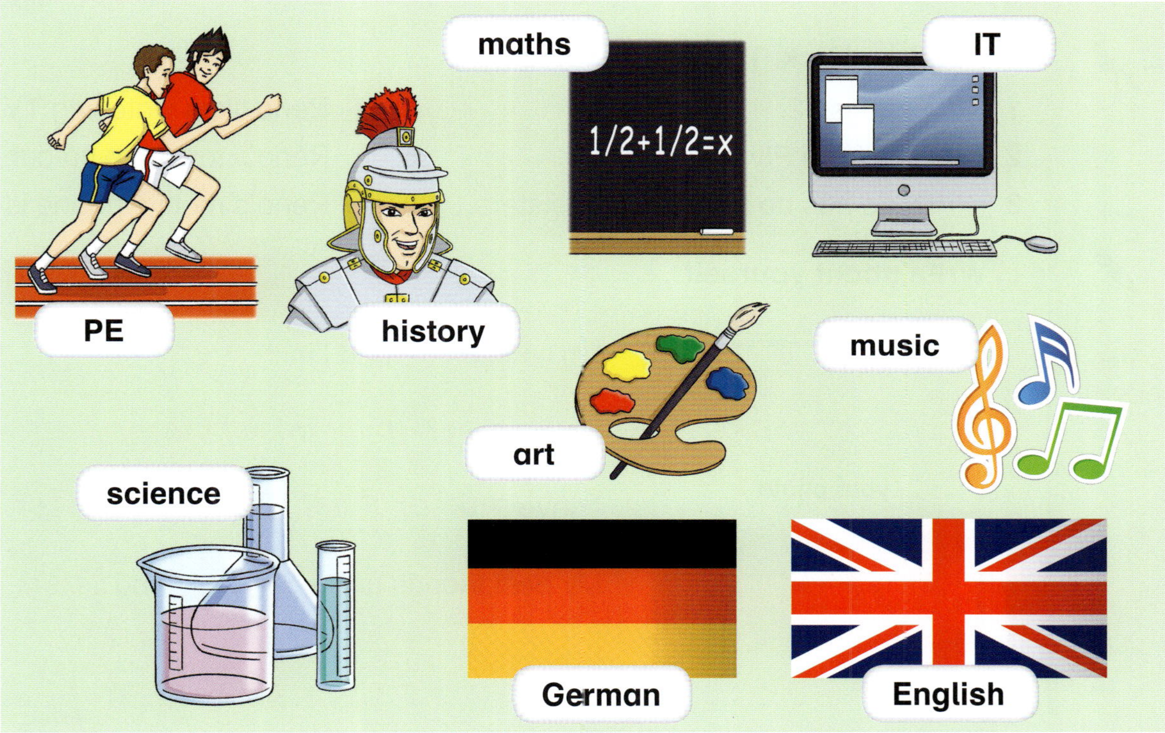

school: ______________________ class: ____ name: __________

	Monday	Tuesday	Wednesday	Thursday	Friday
1					
2					
3					
4					
5					
6					

► SB LH / HD / HL, p. 20–21

6 a) Read about Reno.

I'm Reno and I'm ten.
I'm from London in England.
I have no brothers and sisters.
My best friends are Ali and Sam.
I like watching TV.
I don't like swimming.
I have a dog and two birds.
My favourite lessons are English, art and maths.
My favourite colour is orange.
My favourite thing is my mobile.
It's new and black.

b) Read and tick. True (✓) or false (✗)?

1 ✗ Reno is 12.
2 ✗ He's from Plymouth.
3 ✓ Reno has no brothers and sisters.
4 ✓ Reno likes watching TV.
5 ✗ Reno's favourite colour is red.
6 ✓ Reno's mobile phone is black.

c) Write about yourself[1].

Lösungsbeispiel

your photo

I'm Marie and I'm eleven.
I'm from Berlin in Germany.
I have one brother and one sister.
My best friends are Jenny and Lucy.
I like dancing.
I don't like football.
I have no pets.
My favourite lessons are English and history.
My favourite colour is red.
My favourite thing is my mobile. It's green.

Verwende Renos Text als Muster: Ersetze die grünen Wörter durch deine eigenen Ideen.

d) Compare with a partner.

1 about yourself: *über dich selbst*

▸ SB LH / HD / HL, p. 8–21

7 a) Read and write.

b) Colour the boxes: he, she, it, or they.

he • she • it • they

blue: Adam, Luca; pink: Ms Lee, Ellie, Berry; green: tie, football, pen; yellow: Adam and Luca, students

Ms Lee	she
Adam	he
Berry	she
tie	it
Ellie	she
football	it
Luca	he
Adam and Luca	they
students	they
pen	it

8 a) Look and number.

b) Read and write.

(A)

6

(B)

1

(C)

3

(D)

2

(E)

4

(F)

5

1 This is **Adam**. He has a football.

2 This is **Berry**. She has a pony.

3 This is **a tie**. It's red and yellow.

4 This is **Ellie**. She has a mobile.

5 This is **a football**. It's red and white.

6 This is **Luca**. He has a bike.

9 Read and circle.

1 Ms Lee (is) the English teacher.
Ms Lee isn't the English teacher.

2 Adam and Luca (are) students at Eggy.
Adam and Luca aren't students at Eggy.

3 Cyril: "I'm a bird."
Cyril: "(I'm not) a bird. I'm a crab."

4 Cyril and Sandy (aren't) teachers. They are animals.
Cyril and Sandy are teachers.

► SB LH / HD, pp. 22–23; HL, pp. 28–29

10 Read and draw lines.

I am	I'm
it is	she's
she is	they're
we are	he's
they are	it's
he is	we're
you are	you're

11 Read and write.

's (3x) • 're (2x)

1 Eggy is my new school. It_'s_ big.
2 Ellie is a new girl at Eggy. She_'s_ cool!
3 Adam and Berry aren't here. They_'re_ in the canteen.
4 Berry and I are friends. We_'re_ in class 7Y.
5 Mr Brown is nice. He_'s_ our ICT teacher.
6 Mrs Ford is a teacher too. She_'s_ our art teacher.

12 Read and circle.

1 Eggy isn't / aren't a girl. It's a school.
2 Cyril is a crab. He isn't / aren't a bird.
3 Luca and Adam isn't / aren't girls. They are boys.
4 Ms Lee isn't / aren't the maths teacher. She's the English teacher.

▸ SB LH / HD, pp. 22–23; HL pp. 28–29

13 Complete the network.

English • maths • teacher • principal • ~~rubber~~ • ruler • art • PE • friends • student • pencil sharpener • pen • pencil

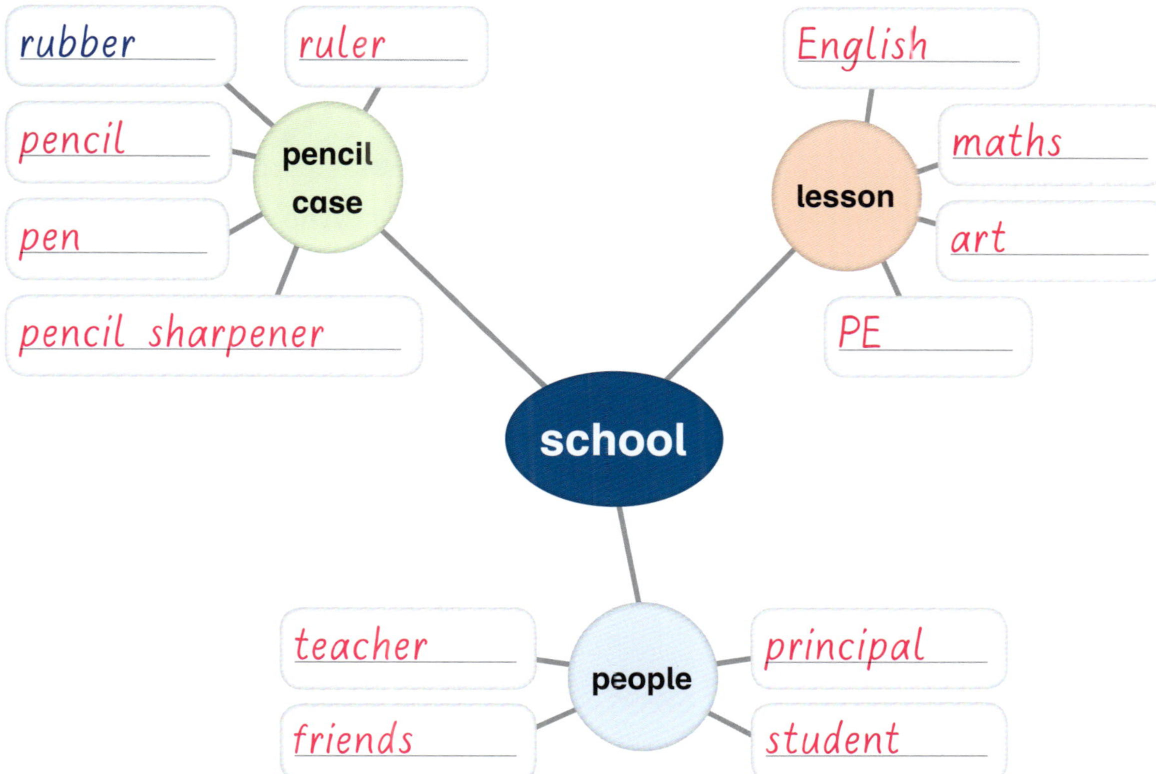

14 Learn new words.

1. Suche dir fünf schwierige Wörter aus dieser Unit aus und schreibe sie auf Karteikarten. Auf die eine Seite schreibst du das englische Wort, auf die andere Seite die deutsche Bedeutung.
2. Wenn du lernst, schau dir zuerst die englische Seite an.
3. Schau dir dann die deutsche Seite an. Schreibe die englische Bedeutung auf.
4. Drehe die Karte um und lies das englische Wort. Alles richtig geschrieben? Wenn nicht, korrigiere deine Fehler.

► SB LH / HD, p. 27; HL p. 25

15 a) Read and number.

3 Sure, here you are, Emma.

1 I'm Tom. What's your name?

5 I like Ms Lee. She's great.

2 I'm Emma. Can I borrow a rubber, please?

4 Thanks. Who's your favourite teacher?

6 I like Ms Lee too.

b) Write the dialogue and underline the green words from 15 a).

Tom: .... I'm Tom. What's your name?
Emma: .... I'm Emma. Can I borrow a rubber, please?
Tom: .... Sure, here you are, Emma.
Emma: .... Thanks. Who's your favourite teacher?
Tom: .... I like Ms Lee. She's great.
Emma: .... I like Ms Lee too.

c) Change the underlined words and act your dialogue.

16 Look and match.

A

B

C

D

E

1 Write six sentences. C
2 Listen and repeat. E
3 Ask your partner. A
4 Read the story. B
5 Look at the pictures. D

► SB LH / HD, p. 28; HL, p. 26

1 Look and write.

~~science~~ • maths • PE • English • three • two

Lesson	Monday	Tuesday
1	$3^2+4^2=5^2$	
2		
3		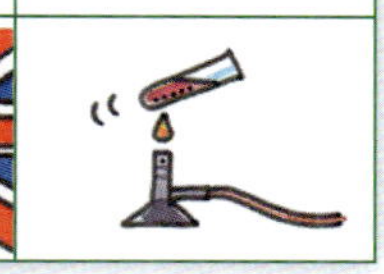

1 Lesson three on Tuesday is science.
2 Lesson one on Monday is maths.
3 Lesson two on Monday is history.
4 Lesson two on Tuesday is PE.
5 Lesson three on Monday is English.
6 Lesson one on Tuesday is English.

2 a) Listen, look and number.

7

b) Read and draw lines.

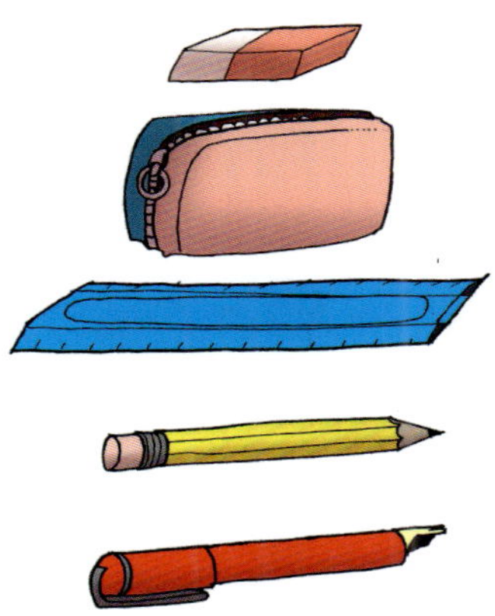

4 – rubber
5 – pencil case
2 – ruler
1 – pencil
3 – pen

pencil
pen
ruler
rubber
pencil case

3 a) Find the words and circle.

b) Write the German words.

l	e	x	e	r	c	i	s	e	l
i	b	o	o	k	a	c	t	y	b
o	r	z	t	a	l	m	p	w	v
k	e	j	d	f	c	h	o	s	c
m	a	q	c	v	u	g	u	y	x
w	k	x	c		l	u	n	c	h
r	v	u	m	n	a	b	d	e	t
i	m	p	o	r	t	a	n	t	q
u	o	l	k	j	o	h	g	f	d
z	t	r	e	w	r	q	a	s	d

wichtig • Schulheft • ~~Pause~~ • Mittagessen • Taschenrechner • Pfund

1 break – Pause
2 calculator – Taschenrechner
3 pound – Pfund
4 important – wichtig
5 exercise book – Schulheft
6 lunch – Mittagessen

4 Read and draw lines.

1 Where's your bike?
2 How are you?
3 Can I borrow a rubber?
4 Who are you?
5 What's your favourite lesson?

A I'm Daniel Green.
B It's at home.
C It's ICT.
D I'm fine, thanks.
E Sure, here you are.

5 Read and circle.

1 Hello. – Hi. / Bye.
2 What's your name? – I'm eleven. / I'm Tom.
3 What's your favourite colour? – A fish. / Red.
4 Where's your tie? – It's blue and white. / It's at home.
5 Can I borrow a pen? – Sure, here you are. / I have a ruler.

6 a) What do you like? What don't you like? Write.

cats • reading • birds • watching TV

Lösungsbeispiel

1 *I like watching TV*.
2 *I don't like birds*.
3 *I like cats*.
4 *I don't like reading*.

b) Compare with a partner.

At home with Ellie

1 Look and draw lines.

1 

2 

3 

4 

A garden

B toilet

C flat

D bathroom

E living room

F house

G bedroom

H kitchen

5 

6 

7 

8 

2 a) Look at the two flats and write.

kitchen • ~~bedroom for the baby~~ • living room • toilet • bedroom • bathroom

b) Read and tick the right picture.

living room

toilet

kitchen

A ☐ 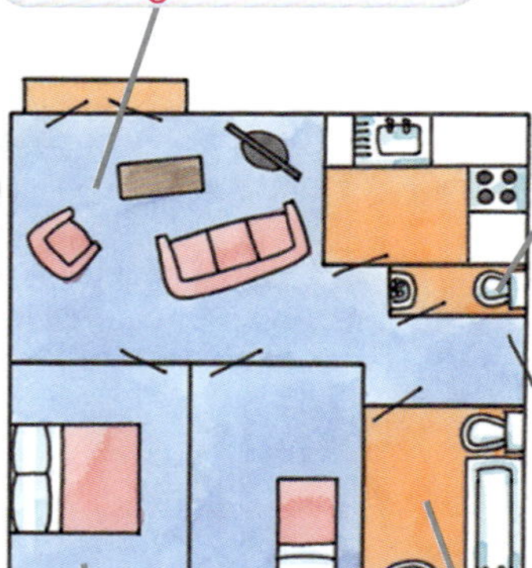

B ☑ 

We have a new flat! It has a living room, a small kitchen, two big bedrooms and a small bedroom (for the baby).

bedroom

bathroom

bedroom for the baby

▸ SB LH / HD / HL, pp. 34–35

3 Look and number.

1	This is me.
2	This is my mum.
7	This is my grandpa.
4	This is my stepsister.
3	This is my stepdad.
5	This is my stepbrother.
6	This is my grandma.

4 a) Read.

This is my family.
This is my sister.
Her name is Sarah. She's 12.
This is my brother.
His name is Tom. He's 17.

b) Write and talk about your family.

Lösungs-beispiel

dad • mum • stepdad • stepmum • brother • sister • stepbrother • stepsister • grandma • grandpa

He • She • His • Her

1 This is my *sister*.
Her name is *Nora*.
She's *9*.

2 This is my *stepbrother*.
His name is *Jim*.
He's *18*.

1 your photo

2 your photo

► SB LH / HD / HL, p. 36–37

8 **5** Listen and draw lines.

6 a) Look and write.

table • shoe • lamp • chair • ~~bed~~ • poster

1 *bed* 2 *lamp* 3 *shoe*

4 *table* 5 *chair* 6 *poster*

b) Look at the room and read. Circle the right words.

I like my bedroom. It's blue and red / green.
I have a bed and a yellow / green chair.
I have a small table with a lamp / mobile.
I have a big flat / table too.
I have five / seven posters.

7 a) Listen and colour.

9

b) Read and colour.

1 The bag is red.

2 The exercise book is orange.

3 The T-shirt is yellow.

4 The book is grey.

8 Look and write.

She's cute • ~~It's too noisy~~ • It's messy • She's lucky

1

2

3

4

1 It's too noisy.

2 She's cute.

3 She's lucky.

4 It's messy.

9 Find the words and circle.

~~unhappy~~ • tired • happy • cool • stupid

unhappystupidcoolhappytired

► SB LH / HD / HL, pp. 38–39

10 Read and write.

he • she • they

1 Is **Conor** Ellies brother? Yes, he is.

2 Are **Luca and Adam** Ellie's friends? Yes, they are.

3 Are **Berry, Adam, Luca and Ellie** in Class 7E? No, they aren't.

4 Is **Berry** Ellie's sister? No, she isn't.

5 Is **Cyril** Ellie's crab? No, he isn't.

11 a) Listen and number.

10

b) Look and write.

he • she • is • isn't • Yes • No

A Is Henry OK? No, he isn't.

B Is Bill OK? Yes, he is.

C Is Mary OK? No, she isn't.

D Is Susan OK? Yes, she is.

E Is Bob OK? No, he isn't.

F Is Jim OK? Yes, he is.

G Is Joey OK? No, he isn't.

12 Ask your partner and tick his or her answers.

1 Is school OK?	☐ Yes, it is.	☐ No, it isn't.
2 Is English OK?	☐ Yes, it is.	☐ No, it isn't.
3 Are your teachers nice?	☐ Yes, they are.	☐ No, they aren't.

► SB LH / HD, pp. 40–41; HL pp. 46–47

13 Listen and write.

Yes, I am • No, I'm not • Are you OK

14 Write about yourself. Then ask a partner.

Yes, I am. • No, I'm not.

1 Are you happy? ______

2 Are you messy? ______

3 Are you tired? ______

15 a) Read and draw lines.

1 Is **Ellie's school** in Germany?	A No, **he** isn't.
2 Are **you** a football fan?	B Yes, **she** is.
3 Is **Luca** your friend?	C No, **it** isn't.
4 Is **Ms Lee** your teacher?	D Yes, **we** are.
5 Are **you and your** sister at Eggy?	E Yes, **I** am.

b) Read and write about yourself.

1 Is your school in Germany? Yes, it is.
Yes, it is. • No, it isn't.

2 Are you a football fan? Yes, I am.
Yes, I am. • No, I'm not.

3 Is Luca your friend? No, he isn't.
Yes, he is. • No, he isn't.

4 Is Ms Lee your teacher? No, she isn't.
Yes, she is. • No, she isn't.

5 Are your teachers OK? Yes, they are.
Yes, they are. • No, they aren't.

► SB LH / HD, pp. 40–41; HL, pp. 46–47

16 The mobile numbers are wrong. Listen and write.

12

1

2

077 9 4 19 9 4 515

077 8 51 819 4 32

17 Listen and number.

13

A

6

B

1

C

4

D

5

E

3

F

2

18 Read and draw lines.

1	Look and write.
2	Listen and write.
3	Listen and circle.
4	Read and tick.
5	Read and write.
6	Look and draw lines.

A	Höre zu und kreise ein.
B	Sieh hin und ziehe Verbindungslinien.
C	Sieh hin und schreibe.
D	Lies und hake ab.
E	Höre zu und schreibe.
F	Lies und schreibe.

► SB LH, pp. 45–46; HD / HL, pp. 43–44

19 a) Look and say.

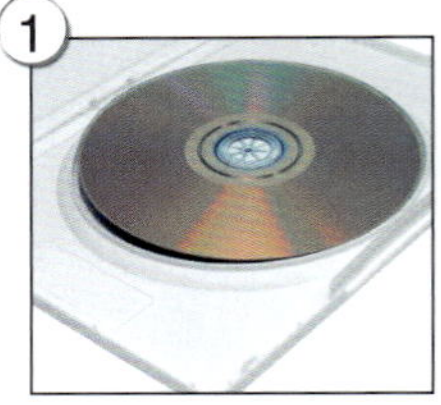

1 a DVD

2 the EU

3 the USA

4 a TV

5 a WC

14 **b) Listen and check. Were you right?**

15 **20 a) Listen and circle.**

Ellie: From Monday to Friday I live in a (flat) / house with my dad, (Alisha) / mum and the baby.

Adam: What's it like?

Ellie: It's (nice) / tired. There are two bedrooms and a big kitchen / (living room). The bathroom is yellow.

Adam: Yellow?! Is your (bedroom) / toilet nice?

Ellie: Mmm … it's OK … it's (pink) / blue! It isn't very big and it's messy, but I like it.

Adam: My garden / (bedroom) is messy too! My (football) / homework things are all over the place.

b) Read with a partner.

c) Write a dialogue with a partner.

Lösungsbeispiel

You: I live in a flat (flat / house) with my mum and dad (mum / dad / sister / brother / ...).

Partner: What's it like?

You: It's (’s / isn't) nice.

There are two (two / three / four) bedrooms and a big (small / big) kitchen.

Partner: Is your bedroom nice?

You: Yes, it is (Yes, it is / No, it isn't).

It's white (white / yellow / pink...).

d) Act the dialogue with your partner.

► SB LH / HD, p. 46; HL, p. 44

1 a) Look and write.

kitchen • lamp • garden • toilet • ~~table~~ • chair • bathroom

1

2

3

			1 t	a	b	l	e		
2 k	i	t	c	h	e	n			
		3 g	a	r	d	e	n		
	4 c	h	a	i	r				
5 b	a	t	h	r	o	o	m		
				6 t	o	i	l	e	t
			7 l	a	m	p			

4

5

6

7

b) Write the word from the blue boxes. _ _ _ _ _ _ _

2 a) Listen and colour.

16

1

2

b) Look and write.

His • Her

1 Ryan's ruler is brown.
2 Kate's bag is red.
3 Her ruler is orange.
4 His bag is blue.
5 Her rubber is green and white.
6 His rubber is white and pink.
7 Her pencil case is pink.

3 Look and write.

dog • crab • cat • ~~elephants~~

's • 're

1 I don't like  elephants. They're too big!

2 My sister has a  dog, Susie. She's black and white.

3 "I love you,  cat! You're old, but I love you!"

4 Cyril is a  crab. He's cute.

4 a) Read about Ben.

name:	Ben Williams
age:	10
brothers, sisters:	one sister (3)
pets:	cat (Molly)
hobbies:	swimming
favourite lesson:	PE
phone numbers:	55643

Hi! My name is Ben Williams. I'm 10.
I have one sister. She's 3.
I have a cat. Her name is Molly. I like swimming.
My favourite lesson is PE.
My phone number is 55643.

b) Now you. Write about yourself.

Lösungs-beispiel

name:	
age:	
brothers, sister:	
pets:	
hobbies:	
favourite lesson:	
phone number:	

Hi! My name is Sarah.
I'm 11. I have one brother.
He's 5.
I have a dog. I like football.
My favourite lesson is English.
My phone number is 4914339.

your photo

My Plymouth[1]

1 Look and write.

~~shopping centre~~ • cinema • swimming pool • park • restaurant • school

In town

1

shopping centre

2

school

3

swimming pool

4

cinema

5

park

6

restaurant

2 Read and write.

1 I live | Plymouth. | in

I live in Plymouth.

2 ride | my bike. | I sometimes

I sometimes ride my bike.

3 go | I often | swimming.

I often go swimming.

4 often go | I | to the cinema.

I often go to the cinema.

▸ SB LH / HD / HL, pp. 52–53

1 in EG HL: Luca's birthday

3 Read and write about Ellie's weekend.

In the morning In the afternoon In the evening	I	sometimes usually always	meet my friends. ride my bike. go to the cinema. go swimming. do my homework.

Lösungs-beispiel

1 *In the morning I usually go swimming.*

2 *In the afternoon I always ride my bike.*

3 *In the evening I sometimes meet my friends.*

4 *In the evening I sometimes go to the cinema.*

4 Read and draw lines.

1 I want to buy sweets.

2 I want to buy jeans and trainers.

3 I want to buy a shirt and a tie.

5 a) Read and circle.

Mum: ...... Look, Ellie. What about the pink **shirt** / week?

Ellie: .... Oh no, Mum! You know I don't like **pink** / present.
But I banana / **like** the blue shirt.

Mum: ...... Yes, but it's too **expensive** / happy – it's £45!

Ellie: .... What about the trainers when / **then**?
I like the red **trainers** / place.

Mum: ...... Mmm, they're OK. But I like the pink trainers.

Ellie: .... Oh Mum! They're tired / **terrible**.

b) Read with a partner.

► SB LH / HD / HL, pp. 54–55

6 Find the words and circle.

a	s	d	p	w	f	s	x	c	v	b	n	m
r	p	a	r	t	y	u	s	w	e	e	k	j
t	z	u	e	i	o	r	p	d	f	g	h	a
f	g	h	s	k	l	p	a	r	e	n	t	s
a	d	c	e	v	b	r	q	w	r	t	z	u
c	q	l	n	j	b	i	r	t	h	d	a	y
t	e	x	t	g	f	s	e	t	u	i	o	p
m	e	s	s	a	g	e	b	g	w	s	d	f

~~present~~ • surprise • text message • parents • party • birthday • week

7 Look and draw lines.

1 

2 

3 

4 

5 

A On my birthday I often go swimming.

B On my birthday I sometimes go to a restaurant.

C On my birthday I always have a party.

D On my birthday I often meet my friends.

E On my birthday I sometimes go to the cinema.

▸ SB LH / HD / HL, p. 56

17 8 Listen and draw lines.

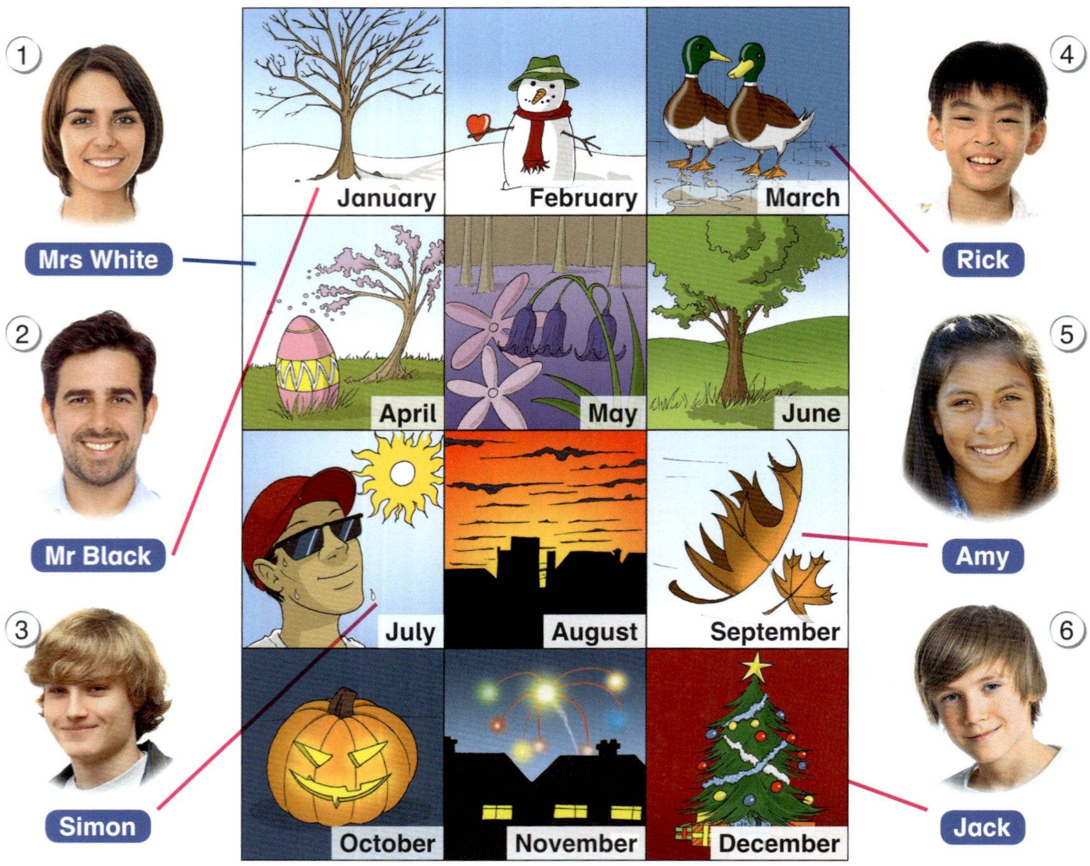

18 9 Listen and circle the months.

JANUARYFEBRUARYMARCHAPRILMAYJUNEJULY
AUGUSTSEPTEMBEROCTOBERNOVEMBERDECEMBER

10 Now you? Write about yourself.

Lösungs-
beispiel

How old are you? I'm 11.

When is your birthday? My birthday is in December.

11 Read and draw lines.

It's on the second of December	2 Dec	It's on the third of November.
It's on the fifteenth of June.	15 Jun	It's on the thirty-first of January.
	31 Jan	
	3 Nov	

► SB LH / HD / HL, p. 57

12 a) Read about Luca and circle.

My best friend Luca

1 Luca (likes) / goes Plymouth.
2 He wants / (lives) with his mum, his dad, Jack and Grace.
3 They (live) / go in Windsor Street.
4 He often (goes) / has to Phone 4U.
5 They (have) / get up all the new mobile phones.
6 Luca and Jack live / (like) their bikes.
7 They (ride) / do their bikes at the weekend.

b) Read the text and numbers and write.

verb	verb + (e)s
3 They live in Windsor Street.	1 Luca likes Plymouth.
5 They have all the new mobile phones.	2 He lives with his mum, his dad, Jack and Grace.
6 Luca and Jack like their bikes.	4 He often goes to Phone 4U.
7 They ride their bikes at the weekend.	

13 Write about Berry.

comes • likes • ~~lives~~ • meets • loves • rides

1 Berry lives in Woolwell.
2 She comes to school by bus.
3 She meets her friends at school.
4 Berry likes animals.
5 And she loves her pony, Harry.
6 She rides her pony after school.

► SB LH / HD, pp. 58–59; HL, pp. 64–65

14 Read and circle.

1 Ellie always has / **stays** at home on her birthday.
2 Adam often listens / **has** a party on his birthday.
3 He and his friends **listen** / have to music.
4 Then they **play** / go games.
5 Berry sometimes has / **goes** to the beach with her parents.

15 Act the dialogue with a partner.

always • often • sometimes

go swimming • go to the cinema • go to a restaurant • have a party • meet my friends • stay at home • play games • watch a film

What do you do on your birthday?

I always go to the cinema.

19

16 a) Look and listen.

b) Read and match.

2	He always has breakfast.	3	He sometimes goes to school by bus.
1	Jim gets up early.	4	He often has lunch in school.
7	He sometimes watches TV.	8	Jim always goes to bed at 10 o'clock.
6	In the evening he has dinner.	5	He always does his homework at home.

► SB LH / HD, pp. 58–59; HL, pp. 64–65

17 **a) Look and write what you can see.**
b) Listen and tick the right price.

chairs • lamp • ~~table~~

1 The  table is … a) ☑ £15. b) ☐ £18.

2 The two  chairs are … a) ☐ £22. b) ☑ £25.

3 The  lamp is … a) ☑ £19. b) ☐ £29.

18 **Listen and draw lines.**

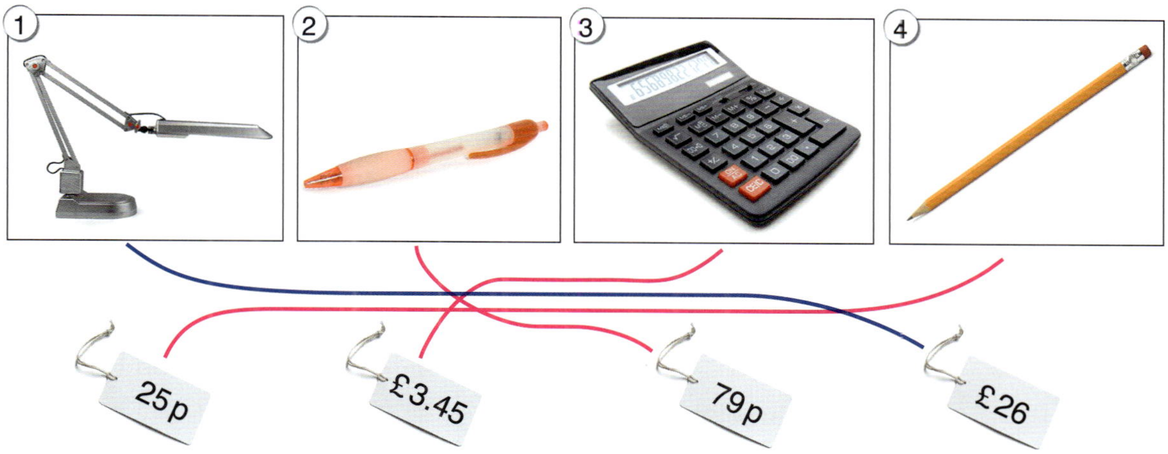

19 **Read, look and talk to a partner.**

our prices			
poster	£1.50	pencil case	£5.50
exercice book	£1.05	ruler	90p

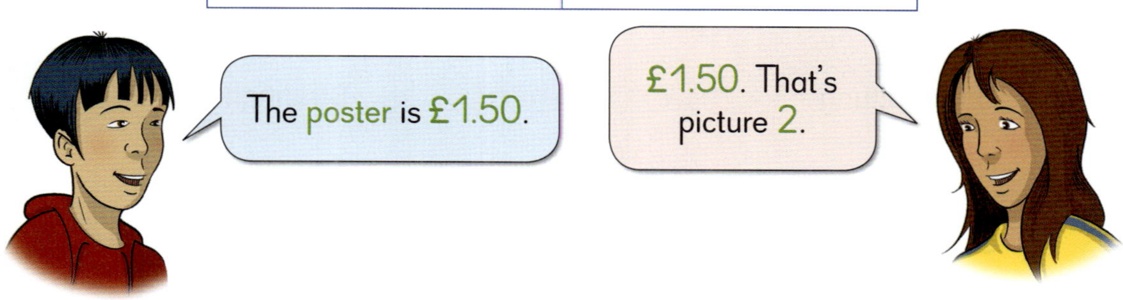

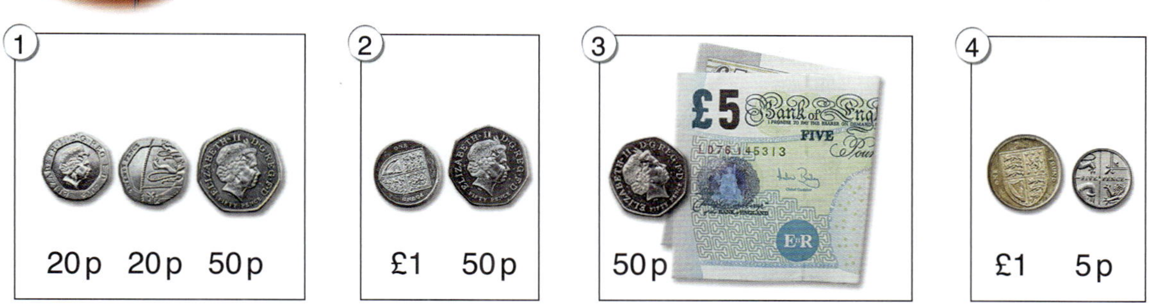

▸ SB LH, pp. 62–63; HD, pp. 64–65; HL, p. 60

20 a) Look and read.

A

B

b) What is it about? Tick.

☐ Rockkonzert	☑ Kosmetik- und Friseursalon
☐ Fußballweltmeisterschaft	☐ Diskothek
☑ Urlaub	☐ Fitnessstudio

21 a) Underline the English words in 20 a.

b) Write the English words next to the German words.

pauschal	– all-inclusive	Mode	– Fashion
kurzfristig	– Last-Minute	Schönheit	– Beauty
Unterhaltung	– Entertainment	Strähnchen	– Highlights
Nachtleben	– Nightlife	Schminke	– Make-up
Schwimmbäder	– Pools	Nägel	– Nails

22 What English words do you use when you speak German? Write.

Lösungsbeispiel

cool, computer, laptop, game, ...

► SB LH, p.64; HD, p.66; HL, p.62

1 Look and write.

garden • ~~toilet~~ • flat • bathroom • living room • house • kitchen • bedroom

1 
toilet

2 
living room

3 
bedroom

4 
bathroom

5 
house

6 
garden

7 
kitchen

8 
flat

2 Write about the birthdays in your family.

Lösungs-beispiel

1 My birthday is in February.

2 My mum's birthday is in March.

3 My dad's birthday is in September.

4 My grandma's birthday is in May.

January • February • March • April • May • June • July • August • September • October • November • December

sister's • brother's • grandma's • grandpa's

3 Read and draw lines.

1	2	3	4	5
seven o'clock	four o'clock	three o'clock	twelve o'clock	one o'clock

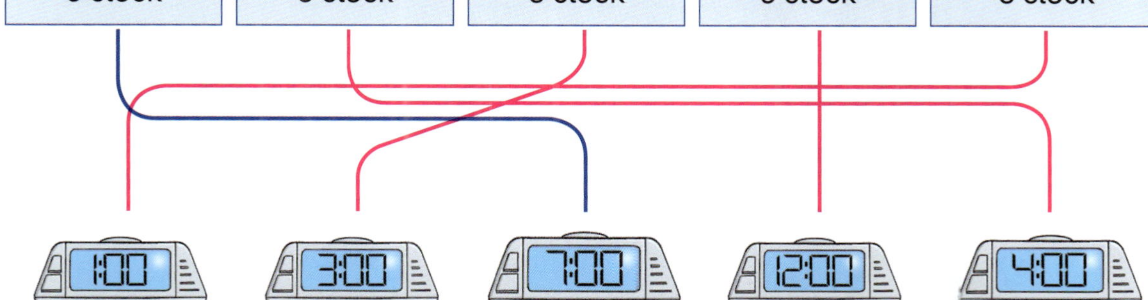

STOP AND PRACTISE

4 Read and draw lines.

1 On Ellie's birthday	A my blue bike to school.
2 In town I sometimes	B she often meets her friends.
3 On my birthday I	C gets up early.
4 I sometimes ride	D always have a party.
5 Rick always	E go to the cinema.

5 Read and tick.

1 Is **your uniform** nice?	☑ No, it isn't.	☐ No, they aren't.
2 Is **Ms Lee** your English teacher?	☐ Yes, we are.	☑ No, she isn't.
3 Are **Ruby and Charlie** in your class?	☑ No, they aren't.	☐ Yes, she is.
4 Are **you** in Zoe's class?	☑ No, I'm not.	☐ Yes, he is.
5 Is **Luca** your friend?	☑ No, he isn't.	☐ Yes, they are.

6 Write about your day.

Lösungs-beispiel

1 

I always get up at *6 o'clock*.

6 • 7 • 8 … o'clock

2 

I *always* have breakfast.

sometimes • often • always

3 

I *go to school by bike*.

walk to school • go to school by bus • go to school by bike

4 

In the afternoon I *often* do my homework.

sometimes • often • always

5 

In the evening I *often* watch TV.

sometimes • often • always

Berry's world[1]

22 **1 Listen and draw lines.**

1 mooh! — cows
2 baah! — sheep
3 miaow! — cats
4 oink! — pigs

pigs
cows
sheep
cats

2 a) Look and write.

sheep • pigs • ~~farm~~ • children • cows • chickens

Lösungs-
beispiel

1 
2 
3 
4 
5 
6 

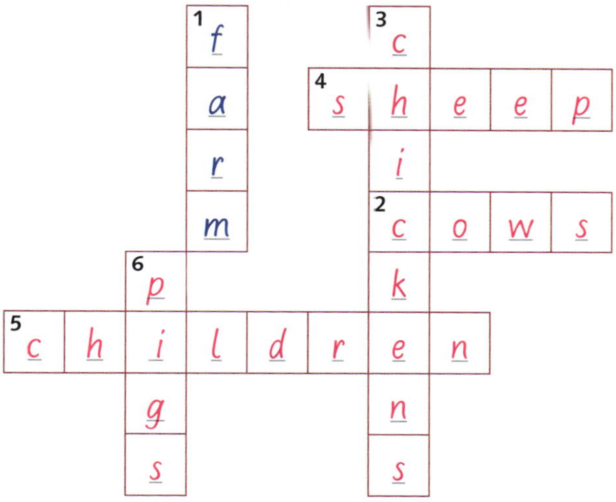

b) Read and write the words from 2 a.

1 Everybody loves Merryweather farm (1).

2 The cows (2) are black and white.

3 You can see cats, dogs, and chickens (3) in Pets Corner.

4 Visitors watch the sheep (4).

5 Children (5) love the pets.

6 Then go and see the pigs (6).

▸ SB LH / HD, pp. 70–71; HL, pp. 72–73

1 in EG HL: Berry's farm

3 Look and draw lines.

1

2

3

4

5

A Berry comes home before 4 o'clock. Then she does her homework.

B At 7 o'clock in the evening she looks after the animals.

C Sam wakes Berry at 6 o'clock in the morning.

D Before breakfast she feeds her pony.

E After breakfast Berry goes to school by car.

4 Read about Luca's family and circle.

1 Mrs Boateng wakes / looks Luca at 7 o'clock.
2 Before breakfast Luca does / looks after his sister Grace.
3 He often rides / watches his bike to school.
4 At school he likes / goes English and sport.
5 He gets / wakes home at about 3.45.
6 He does / goes his homework.
7 Sometimes he rides / watches TV.
8 He likes / goes to bed at about 9.30.

▸ SB LH / HD, p. 72; HL p. 74

23 5 a) Listen and write.

12:45 • 5:15 • 6:00 • ~~7:15~~ • 8:00 • 9:45 • 8:30

1

2

3

4

5

6

7

b) Talk to a partner.

Partner A: Point to a time in a) and ask.

What's the time?

Partner B: Say the time.

It's 8 o'clock.

24 6 a) Listen and circle.

first lesson	9.00 / 9.30	to 10.00
second lesson	9.45 / 10.00	to 11.00
third lesson	11.25 / 11.40	to 12.25
fourth lesson	12.25 / 12.20	to 1.25

b) Talk to a partner about your school.

When's our first lesson?

Our first lesson? It's from 8.00 to 8.45.

And when's our second lesson?

► SB LH / HL, pp. 73; HD, p. 75

7 Read and circle what is true for you.

Lösungsbeispiel

1 I feel great / (fed up) when I have lots of homework.
2 I feel (great) / fed up when I go swimming.
3 I feel great / (fed up) when I can't meet my friends.
4 I feel great / (fed up) when my friends borrow my things.
5 I feel great / (fed up) when our class has PE.
6 I feel (great) / fed up when I can watch TV.

8 a) Read and write about Adam.

	Time	Activity	Feeling
1	8.00	I like breakfast!	☺
2	10.00	I have art. Art is boring.	☹
3	11.00	I have PE. I like that.	☺
4	2.00	I like maths. It's OK.	😐
5	6.00	I do my homework.	☹
6	8.00	I watch TV.	☺

great • fed up • OK

1 At 8 o'clock Adam feels great because he likes breakfast.
2 At 10 o'clock he feels fed up because he has an art lesson.
3 At 11 o'clock he feels great because he has PE.
4 At 2 o'clock he feels OK because he likes maths.
5 At 6 o'clock he feels fed up because he does his homework.
6 At 8 o'clock he feels great because he watches TV.

b) Write about yourself.

Lösungsbeispiel

	Time	Activity	Feeling
1	7.00	I have breakfast!	☺
2	10.00	I have PE.	☺
3	5.00	I do my homework.	☹

1 At 7 o'clock I feel great because I have breakfast.
2 At 10 o'clock I feel great because I have PE.
3 At 5 o'clock I feel fed up because I do my homework.

▸ SB LH / HL, pp. 74–75; HD, pp. 76–77

9 a) Look and write.

lamp • chair • bed • ~~TV~~ • computer • ~~table~~ • toilet • poster

doesn't

1 Jack's bedroom has a *table* but it *doesn't* have a *TV*.

2 His bedroom has a *chair* but it *doesn't* have a *computer*.

3 His bedroom has a *bed* but it *doesn't* have a *toilet*.

4 His bedroom has a *poster* but it *doesn't* have a *lamp*.

b) Write about your bedroom.

Lösungsbeispiel

1 My bedroom has a *computer* but it *doesn't* have a *TV*.

2 It has a *bed* but it *doesn't* have a *chair*.

c) Write what you do and what you don't do in your bedroom.

~~listen to music~~ • read • dance • ~~watch TV~~ • play football • do my homework • play games • ride a bike

don't

Lösungsbeispiel

1 I *listen to music* but I *don't watch TV* in my bedroom.

2 I *play games* but I *don't play football* in my bedroom.

3 I *dance* but I *don't ride a bike* in my bedroom.

10 Read and write about Ellie's family.

~~doesn't live~~ • doesn't miss • don't have • don't ask

1 Ellie *doesn't live* with her mum at weekends – she lives with her dad.

2 She *doesn't miss* her mum. She sees her mum from Monday to Friday.

3 Ellie's dad has a baby with Alisha. But Ellie's mum and Pete *don't have* a baby.

4 Alisha and Steve often go to a restaurant. They *don't ask* Ellie to come too.

11 a) Read and draw lines.

1 What do you do in the evenings, Ellie?

2 When do you go to bed?

3 Where is your bedroom?

4 Do you like your bedroom?

A Yes, I like my bedroom.

B It's upstairs.

C I do my homework or I watch TV.

D At about 9.30.

b) Write about yourself.

1 What do you do in the evenings?	*I*
2 When do you go to bed?	
3 Do you like your bedroom?	

play games • watch TV • do my homework • listen to music • read

At about 8.30 • 9.00 • 9.30 …

Yes, I like my bedroom. • No, I don't like my bedroom.

c) Talk to a partner.

► SB LH, p. 78–79; HD pp. 79–80; HL pp. 82–83

12 Look and write. Where do you find these signs?

on a beach • in a cinema • in a school

1

on a beach

2

in a cinema

3

in a school

14 Read and talk to a partner.

Arbeitet mit einem Partner zusammen. Stellt euch vor, ihr seid im Aquarium und könnt nicht alles verstehen. Stellt euch abwechselnd die folgenden Fragen und versucht sie zu beantworten:

1 Gibt es im Aquarium nur Fische oder auch andere Tiere?
2 Mein Freund sitzt im Rollstuhl. Kann er das Aquarium trotzdem besuchen?
3 Kann man dort auch etwas zu essen kaufen?
4 Hat das Aquarium bis 17 Uhr auf?
5 Könnte ich dort meinen Geburtstag feiern?
6 Was kostet der Eintritt für einen Erwachsenen und ein Kind?

AQUARIUM

- home to fish and other animals
- cafe
- wheelchair friendly
- great for children birthday parties
- prices: Adults (16+) £3.00
  Child (3–15) £2.00
- open 10.00 am–3.45 pm

► SB LH, p.82; HD, p.84; HL, p.78

15 Look and match. Write the numbers.

1

I want to listen to music.

2

I want to watch a film.

3

I want to play games.

4

I want to go to the beach.

A

Please bring a DVD.

B

Please bring a good game.

C

Please bring swimming things.

D

Please bring CDs.

16 a) Read the invitation.

It's my birthday!

Dear David,

Please come to my party.

Where? • 16 King street

When? • Monday, 3rd May

What time? • 4 o'clock to 7 o'clock

I want to go to the beach. Please bring swimming things.

b) Write an invitation to your birthday party.

Lösungs-beispiel

It's my birthday!

Dear Natasha,

Please come to my party.

Where? • Bornholmer Straße 12

When? • Monday, 3rd June

What time? • 3 o'clock to 6 o'clock

I want to watch a film. Please bring a DVD.

► SB LH, p. 83; HD, p. 85; HL, p. 79

1 Look and write.

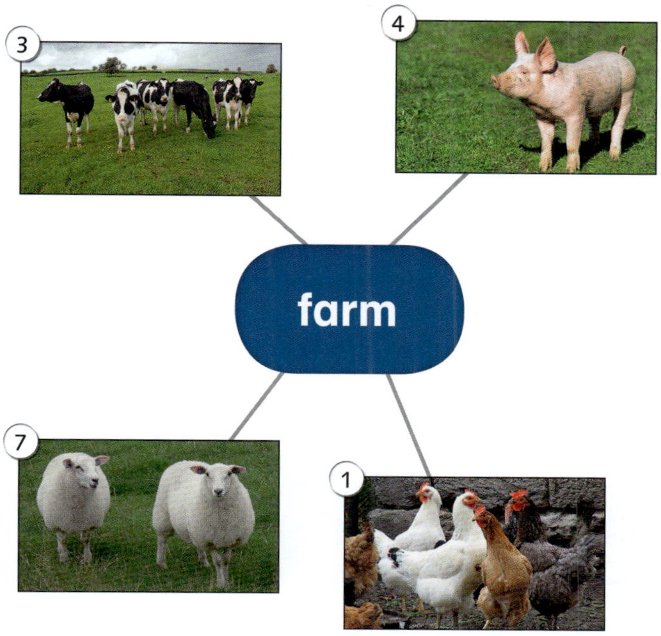

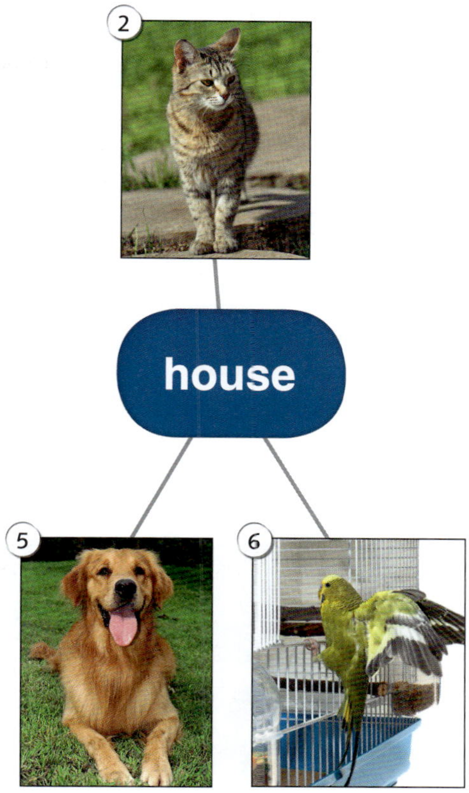

sheep • bird • cows • farm • house • cat • ~~chickens~~ • pig • dog

1 The *chickens* live on the farm.
2 The *cat* lives in the house.
3 The *cows* live on the farm.
4 The *pig* lives on the *farm*.
5 The *dog* lives in the *house*.
6 The *bird* lives in the house.
7 The *sheep* live on the farm.

2 a) Find the words and circle.
b) Write the words.

only • outside • wet • field • left • laugh • ~~shoulder~~

q	e	r	t	z	s	u	o	p
s	d	o	f	g	h	j	k	l
a	s	u	y	c	o	n	l	y
w	e	t	u	p	u	h	a	m
x	v	s	i	o	l	g	u	n
i	f	i	e	l	d	f	g	b
z	t	d			e	a	h	v
r	l	e	f	t	r	y	x	c

1 Schulter – *shoulder*
2 nass – *wet*
3 lachen – *laugh*
4 nur, bloß – *only*
5 links – *left*
6 Feld, Weide – *field*
7 draußen – *outside*

STOP AND PRACTISE

3 Read about Adam and write.

doesn't have • ~~wakes~~ • goes • comes • don't like

1 My mum always wakes me at 6.30.

2 She doesn't have breakfast with me.

3 She goes to work at 6.45.

4 I don't like that.

5 She often comes home after 8.30 in the evening.

4 Look and write about yourself.

Lösungsbeispiel

1 I always get up at 7 o'clock.

2 I have breakfast at 7.30.

3 I go to school at 7.45.

4 I have lunch at 1 o'clock.

5 I do my homework at 4 o'clock.

6 I go to bed at 9 o'clock.

5 Write sentences about you and your family.

I My parents	don't	have lunch at school / home. go to work / school by bus. have a pony / cat / bird / dog. watch football on TV. play games at the weekend.
My sister / brother My grandma / grandpa	doesn't	

Lösungsbeispiel

1 I don't have lunch at school.

2 My parents don't play games at the weekend.

3 My grandma doesn't watch football on TV.

All about Adam

Unit 5

23

1 Listen and circle.

Ellie: .... Are you going home, Adam?
Adam: .... No, I always go to the cafe after school / swimming.
Ellie: .... To the cafe / cinema?
Adam: .... Yeah, my mum / parents have a cafe.
Ellie: .... A cafe? Great! / Cool!
Adam: .... Yeah, it's OK, but it's lots of work in the evenings / summer.
Ellie: .... What do you do at the cafe?
Adam: .... I wash up, I clean[1] the tables / chairs, I clean the kitchen.
Ellie: .... Wow! I do nothing at home!

2 a) Write the words.

summer • ~~boat~~ • beach • crab

o b a t	1 boat	b c e h a	3 beach
r b c a	2 crab	m s e r u m	4 summer

b) Circle what is true for you.

Lösungs-beispiel

1 I like / don't like the summer.

2 Crabs are / aren't my favourite animals.

3 I'm / I'm not excited when I'm on a boat.

4 On the beach I like / don't like reading a book.

3 Look and tick. True (✓) or false (✗)?

1 ✗ There's a crab in the picture.

2 ✓ There are five children.

3 ✗ There are toilets.

4 ✓ There are two small boats.

5 ✗ There's a dog in the picture.

6 ✗ There's a cinema.

1 clean: *sauber machen, putzen*

▸ SB LH, pp. 90–91; HD, pp. 92–93; HL, pp. 88–89

4 a) Look and write.

coffee • water • cream • salad • tea • soup • juice • ~~chips~~

1 
2 
3 
4 
5 
6 
7 
8 

				1 c	h	i	p	s
		2 s	o	u	p			
				3 s	a	l	a	d
				4 t	e	a		
			5 c	o	f	f	e	e
6 c	r	e	a	m				
7 j	u	i	c	e				
8 w	a	t	e	r				

b) Write the word from the blue boxes. _ _ _ _ _ _ _ _

5 Read and draw lines.

1 Adam's mum works	A washes up in the cafe.
2 Adam sometimes	B tired.
3 At school Adam is often	C very happy at school.
4 He often doesn't do	D in a cafe.
5 He isn't	E his homework.

6 a) Look and write.

~~wash up~~ • cook • read books • text • play games • listen to music

1  wash up

2  read books

3  cook

4  text

5 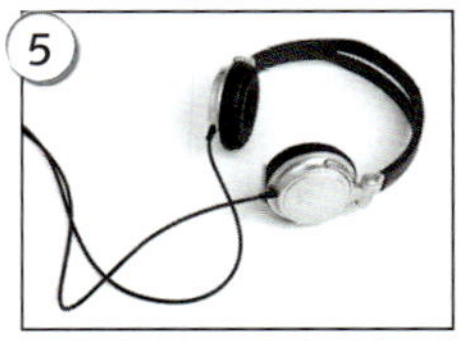 listen to music

6  play games

► SB LH, p. 92; HD, p. 94; HL, pp. 90–91

b) Write about yourself. Then talk to a partner.

Lösungs-
beispiel

1 Do you often listen to music? Yes, I do.

2 Do you sometimes play games? No, I don't.

3 Do you often read books? Yes, I do.

4 Do you sometimes wash up? No, I don't.

5 Do you often text your friends? Yes, I do.

Yes, I do. • No, I don't.

7 **Look and write Adam's list.**

do my homework • phone dad • ~~play the guitar~~ • send a letter to grandpa

This afternoon I must:

1 play the guitar

2 do my homework

3 phone dad

4 send a letter to grandpa

8 **Look and number.**

4 Adam is thinking about school.

5 Conor is reading a book.

3 Zoe is doing her homework.

2 Ellie is texting her dad.

1 Ellie's mum is cooking.

6 Pete is washing up.

▸ SB LH, p. 93; HD, p. 95; HL, p. 91

9 Look and write.

Can you meet me? • You can't • Can you send me • ~~You can't stay here.~~

10 a) Listen and write.

26

pencil • ~~school bag~~ • rubber • ruler

b) Draw lines and write the answers.

1 Can I have your school bag, please?	
2 Can I have your pencil, please?	
3 Can I have your ruler, please?	
4 Can I have your rubber, please?	

	No, you can't.
	Yes, you can.
	Yes, you can.
	No, you can't.

11 Draw three things in the pencil case. Then talk to a partner.

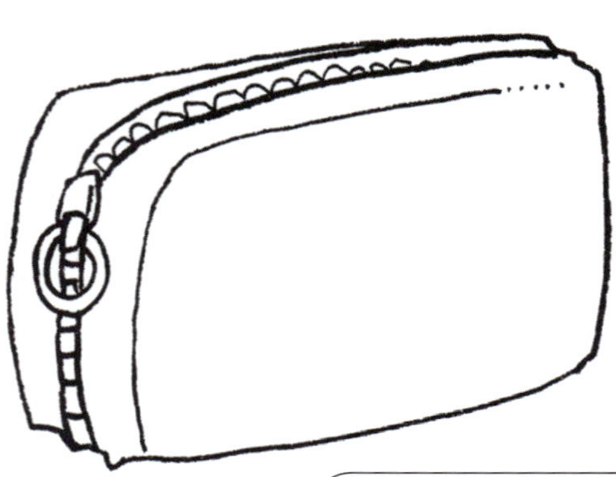

1 dive: *tauchen* 2 brochure: *Prospekt*

▸ SB LH, p. 94; HD, p. 96; HL, p. 92

27 **12 a) Look and listen.**

b) Look and write.

I'm helping mum. • I can't. • ~~I'm doing my homework.~~ • I'm making dinner. • What are you doing?

c) Look and tick. True (✓) or false (✗)?

1 ✗ There are three posters in picture number one.

2 ✓ There's a computer in picture number two.

3 ✓ There are eight books in picture number two.

4 ✗ There's a bus in picture number five.

5 ✗ There are seven children in picture number six.

1 wash: *waschen* **2** help: *helfen* **3** clean: *sauber machen* **4** honey, *hier: Schatz*

▸ SB LH, pp. 96–97; HD, pp. 99–99; HL, p. 88

13 Read and tick what is true for Adam.

1	Do my parents have a cafe?	☺	☑ Yes, they do.	☐ No, they don't.
2	Do I have a sister?	☹	☐ Yes, you do.	☑ No, you don't.
3	Does my mum work in a cinema?	☹	☐ Yes, she does.	☑ No, she doesn't.
4	Do I like music?	☺	☑ Yes, you do.	☐ No, you don't.
5	Do I go to PMZ music club?	☺	☑ Yes, you do.	☐ No, you don't.

14 a) Read about Ellie and draw lines.

b) Check with a partner.

1 Does Ellie like pink?	A No, they don't.
2 Do Ellie's parents live together?	B Yes, they do.
3 Does Ellie live in Plymouth?	C No, she doesn't.
4 Do Ellie and Adam go to Eggy?	D Yes, they do.
5 Do Ellie's dad and Alisha have a baby?	E Yes, she does.

(Lines: 1 – C, 2 – A, 3 – E, 4 – D, 5 – B)

15 a) Write about yourself.

Lösungsbeispiel

1 Do you like pink? *Yes, I do.* — Yes, I do. • No, I don't.

2 Do your parents live together? *No, they don't.* — Yes, they do. • No, they don't.

3 Do you live in Hamburg? *No, I don't.* — Yes, I do. • No, I don't.

b) Talk to a partner.

c) Write your partner's name and circle his or her answers.

Lösungsbeispiel

1 *Daniel* ______ likes / (doesn't like) pink.

2 (His) / Her parents live / (don't live) together.

3 (He) / She ____ lives / (doesn't live) in Hamburg.

► SB LH, pp. 100–101

16 a) **Listen and number.**

Can I have an orange, please?

b) **Talk to a partner.**

Hello. Can I have a sandwich, please?

Here you are.

a drink	**an** orange juice
a cheese sandwich	**a** bottle of water
a soup	**a** tea
a salad	**a** coffee

17 **Listen and write.**

soup of the day	£ 2.50	scone, jam and cream	£3.85
chicken sandwich	£4.50	tea	£1.50
cheese sandwich	£3.95	coffee	£1.90
chips	£7.30	orange juice	£2.10
salad	£4.40	bottle of water	£2.10

£2.10 •
£4.40 •
£1.50 •
~~£3.95~~ •
£7.30

18 a) **Read and write.**

b) **Talk to a partner.**

Lösungs-beispiel

You: .... Can I have a green salad, please?

Partner: .... Here you are. Anything else?

You: .... Yes, a cheese sandwich, please.

Partner: .... Anything else?

You: .... No, thank you, that's all.

Partner: .... That's £5.50, please.

MENU

food	
cheese sandwich	£3.00
salads	
green salad	£2.50
soups	
soup of the day	£3.00
drinks	
orange juice	£2.50

▸ SB LH, p. 96

30 **19 Listen and tick.**

20 a) Look and tick. True (✓) or false (✗)?

1 ✓ On the left I can see a woman.

2 ✓ Next to the woman there's a book.

3 ✓ In the middle there's dog.

4 ✗ Next to the dog there's a cat.

5 ✓ I can see a boat on the water behind the woman.

6 ✗ On the right I can see a bird.

7 ✗ In front of the woman there's a cheese sandwich.

b) Correct the three wrong sentences.

Next to the dog there's a ball.

On the right I can see a woman.

In front of the woman there's a baby.

ball • baby • woman

▸ SB LH, p. 100; HD, p. 102

1 Look and circle.

1 The lamp is under / behind the chair.
2 The table is between / in front of the bed and the chair.
3 The guitar is next to / under the bed.
4 The lamp is next to / behind the poster.
5 The table is behind / next to the bed.

2 a) Find the words and circle.

b) Write.

trouble • soon • sing • angry • proud • difficult • ~~today~~

a	w	t	e	r	t	z	t	h	s
p	r	o	u	d	h	j	r	k	i
g	f	d	s	a	y	s	o	o	n
j	k	a	n	g	r	y	u	c	g
p	o	y	u	s	z	t	b	r	e
d	i	f	f	i	c	u	l	t	w
h	g	m	f	n	d	s	e	a	q

1 heute – t o d a y
2 wütend – a n g r y
3 bald – s o o n
4 schwierig – d i f f i c u l t
5 stolz – p r o u d
6 singen – s i n g
7 Problem – t r o u b l e

3 Trace and write.

pencil case • ~~pencil~~ • book • ruler

1 Can I have your pencil, please?	
2 Can I have your pencil case, please?	
3 Can I have your ruler, please?	
4 Can I have your book, please?	

	Yes, you can.
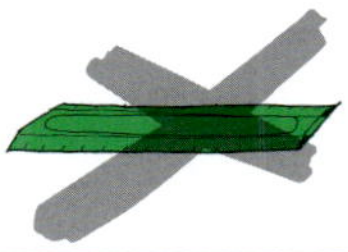	No, you can't.
	Yes, you can.
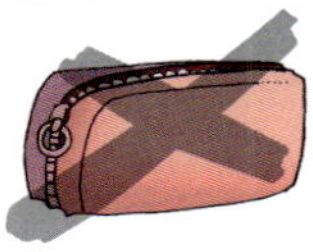	No, you can't.

4 a) **Listen and tick.**

31

	1		2		3		4	
	☺	☹	☺	☹	☺	☹	☺	☹
	☑	☐	☐	☑	☐	☑	☑	☐

b) **Read and write about yourself.**

Lösungsbeispiel

Yes, I do. • No, I don't.

1 Do you like dancing? *Yes, I do.*

2 Do you like swimming? *No, I don't.*

3 Do you like reading? *Yes, I do.*

4 Do you like playing games? *No, I don't.*

5 **Listen and draw lines.**

32

1 

2 

Yes, he does.

Yes, she does.

No, he doesn't.

No, she doesn't.

3 

4 

(1 – Yes, she does. · 2 – No, she doesn't. · 3 – No, he doesn't. · 4 – Yes, she does.)

6 **Tick and write about your friend.**

Lösungsbeispiel

Does your friend …	often	sometimes	never	
a) … listen to you?	☑	☐	☐	My friend *often* listens to me.
b) … text you?	☑	☐	☐	My friend *often* texts me.
c) … give you presents?	☐	☐	☑	My friend *never* gives me presents.

School is out – for summer

1 Complete the network

1 Du behältst neue Wörter leichter, wenn du sie in Gruppen ordnest.
2 Hier geht es um Ferien.
3 Denke darüber nach, wo du deine Ferien verbringen könntest (*Where?*), mit wem (*Who?*) und was du machen könntest (*What?*).
4 Unten findest du Ideen: Möchtest du etwas einfügen, weißt aber nicht wie es heißt? Schau hinten im Wörterverzeichnis nach.

Lösungsbeispiel

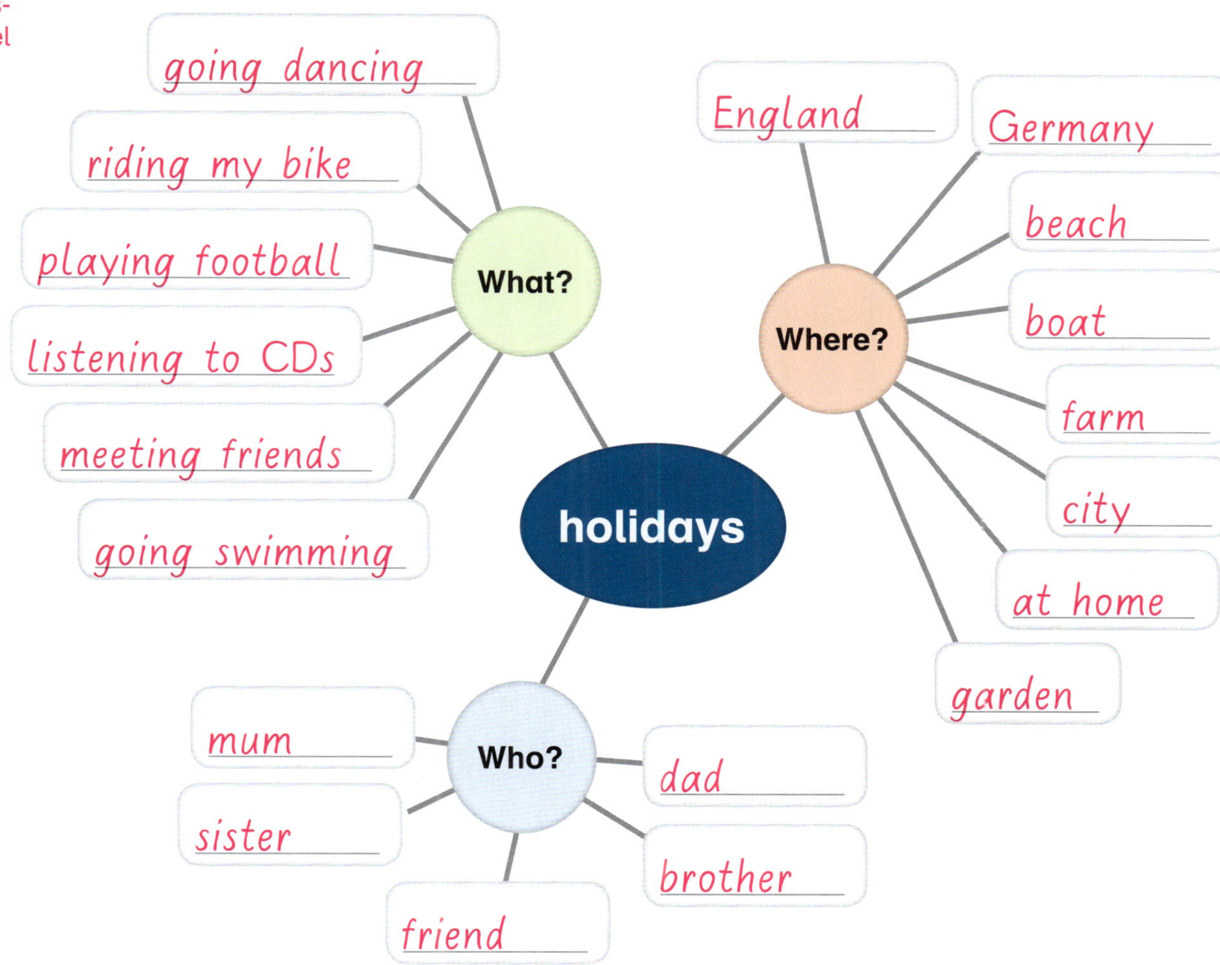

England • Germany • beach • city • boat • farm • at home • garden • mum • dad • sister • brother • friend • going dancing • riding my bike • playing football • listening to CDs • meeting friends • playing games • going swimming

► SB LH, pp. 108–109; HD, p. 110–111

1 Listen and number.

33

A

B

C

D

2 a) Read with a partner.

b) Write a dialogue about your holiday plans.

Lösungs-beispiel

You: .... Hi, Mia. What are you doing in the holidays?

Partner: ... I'm going to England. I'm meeting friends there.

You: .... Who is going with you?

Partner: ... My dad.

You: .... That's cool.

1 Italy: *Italien* **2** visit: *besuchen* **3** aunt: *Tante* **4** uncle: *Onkel*

▸ SB LH, pp. 108 – 109; HD, pp. 110 – 111

Das **Vocabulary** (S. 61–75) enthält alle neuen Wörter und Wendungen des Arbeitsheftes, die du **lernen** musst. Sie stehen in der Reihenfolge, in der sie im Arbeitsheft zum ersten Mal vorkommen.

Hier siehst du, wie das **Vocabulary** aufgebaut ist:

Die **blauen Kästen** solltest du dir immer besonders gut ansehen. Dort stehen wichtige Hinweise zu den neuen Wörtern.

Mit Hilfe der Beispielsätze und Bilder kannst du dir neue Wörter besser merken.

Der **blaue Pfeil** heißt: Zu diesem Eintrag gibt es in der rechten Spalte einen blauen Kasten.

Das **rote Ausrufezeichen** bedeutet: Vorsicht, hier macht man leicht Fehler!

playing games	Spiele spielen	
What are …?	Was sind …? / Welche(s) sind …?	
animal	Tier	
have	haben	
cat	Katze	
bird	Vogel	
an elephant	ein Elefant →	**a – an** **a** dog **an** elephant **a** bird **an** animal
dog	Hund	
different	unterschiedlich, verschieden, anders	
no	kein, keine	We have **no** car. 
he's (= he is)	er ist	
she's (= she is)	sie ist	
I do my homework	ich mache (meine) Hausaufgaben	**!** Englisch: **Homework is** important. Deutsch: **Hausaufgaben sind** wichtig.

Unit 2: At home with Ellie

house	Haus	
flat	Wohnung	
Theme 2		
happy	glücklich, froh	
unhappy	unglücklich	**happy** ◄► **unhappy**
look at	anschauen	

Dies ist das „Gegenteil"-Zeichen. **happy ◄► unhappy** bedeutet: „happy" ist das Gegenteil von „unhappy".

Im **Vocabulary** wird folgende **Abkürzung** verwendet:

pl = *plural* (Mehrzahl)

Wenn du **nachschlagen** möchtest, was ein englisches Wort bedeutet, dann solltest du das **Dictionary** auf den Seiten 76–80 verwenden.

Nice to meet you

Hi!	Hallo.	
What's your name?	Wie heißt du? (*wörtlich:* Was ist dein Name?)	
I'm (= I am)	ich bin	
the crab	der Krebs	
four	vier	→
What about you?	Und du? / Was ist mit dir?	
from Plymouth	aus Plymouth	
in England	in England	
Germany	Deutschland	
partner	Partner/in	one **partner** – two **partners** one **class** – two **classes**
class	(Schul-)Klasse	
game	Spiel	
I can see a crab	ich kann einen Krebs sehen	
and	und	
a beach	ein Strand	
colour	Farbe	
Welcome to Plymouth**.**	Willkommen in Plymouth!	
green	grün	→
red	rot	
yellow	gelb	
brown	braun	
black	schwarz	
blue	blau	
white	weiß	
pink	rosa	
orange	orange	
say	sagen	
like	mögen	
sweets	Bonbons, Süßigkeiten	
I **like** red.	Ich mag Rot.	
I don't like blue.	Ich mag Blau nicht. / Ich mag kein Blau.	
hobby	Hobby	**!** *Englisch*: one **hobby** – two **hobbies** *Deutsch*: ein **Hobby** – zwei **Hobbys**

1 one	**6 six**	**11 eleven**
2 two	**7 seven**	**12 twelve**
3 three	**8 eight**	**13 thirteen**
4 four	**9 nine**	**14 fourteen**
5 five	**10 ten**	

colours: **green** **red** **yellow** **brown** **black** **blue** **white** **pink** **orange**

football	Fußball
watching TV	Fernsehen
too	auch
swimming	Schwimmen
dancing	Tanzen
reading	Lesen
playing games	Spiele spielen
What are ...?	Was sind ...? / Welche(s) sind ...?
animal	Tier
have	haben
cat	Katze
bird	Vogel
an elephant	ein Elefant →
dog	Hund
different	unterschiedlich, verschieden, anders
my	mein/e
favourite thing	Lieblingssache
bike	Fahrrad
it's (= it is)	es ist (*bei Dingen und Tieren auch:* er ist, sie ist)
great	großartig, toll
small	klein
old	alt
but	aber
mobile (phone)	Handy
new	neu
big	groß
the last day of the holidays	der letzte Tag der Ferien
Hello.	Hallo.
It's me.	Ich bin's.
no	nein
yes	ja
go away	weggehen
go	gehen; fahren
stupid	dumm, blöd; albern

a – an
a dog **an** elephant
a bird **an** animal

This is a bike	Dies ist ein Fahrrad / Das ist ein Fahrrad	
help	Hilfe	
Goodbye.	Auf Wiedersehen.	

Unit 1: Welcome to our school

our	unser/e	
at school	in der Schule	**!** *Englisch*: They're **at school**. *Deutsch*: Sie sind **in der Schule**.
boy	Junge	
girl	Mädchen	
teacher	Lehrer/in	
car	Auto	**a car** 
first (= 1st)	erste, erster, erstes	
How are you?	Wie geht's? / Wie geht es dir / euch?	
I'm OK. / I'm fine.	Es geht mir gut.	
thanks	danke	
Bye.	Tschüs.	
good	gut	
See you.	Bis dann. / Tschüs.	

Theme 1

Good morning.	Guten Morgen.	
English	Englisch; englisch	
Who are you?	Wer bist du? / Wer seid ihr?	→ **what?** was? **who?** wer? **how?** wie?
brother	Bruder	
sister	Schwester	
we're (= we are)	wir sind	
best	beste(r, s); am besten	
friend	Freund/in	
they're (= they are)	sie sind	
no	kein, keine	We have **no** car. 
he's (= he is)	er ist	
she's (= she is)	sie ist	
Mr Smith	Herr Smith	
Mrs Smith	Frau Smith	
or	oder	

Theme 2

maths	Mathematik	
here	hier; hierher	
art	Kunst	
PE (physical education)	(Schul-)Sport	
where?	wo? / wohin?	→ **who?** wer? **where?** wo?
he / she / it isn't (= is not)	er / sie / es ist nicht	
lesson	(Unterrichts-)Stunde	
now	nun, jetzt	
timetable	Stundenplan	
time	Zeit; Uhrzeit	
Monday	Montag	
Tuesday	Dienstag	
Wednesday	Mittwoch	
Thursday	Donnerstag	
Friday	Freitag	
music	Musik	
break	Pause	
lunch	Mittagessen	
on Monday	am Montag	What's lesson one **on Monday**?
right	richtig	That's **right**. ✔
wrong	falsch	That's **wrong**. ✘

Story

before	bevor; vor	**before** you read: **bevor** du liest **before** the lesson: **vor** der Stunde
Ellie has …	Ellie hat …	
tie	Krawatte	
principal	Schulleiter/in	
please	bitte	
remember	daran denken, nicht vergessen; sich erinnern an	
important	wichtig	
Sorry. / I'm sorry.	Tut mir leid. / Entschuldigung.	
at home	zu Hause	
That isn't good.	Das ist nicht gut.	
know	wissen; kennen	

Look, Adam.	Sieh mal, Adam. / Schau mal, Adam.	
bad	schlecht; schlimm	**good ◂▸ bad**
idea	Idee	
people	Leute, Menschen	
think	denken, meinen, glauben	
Ellie's tie	Ellies Krawatte	

Skills training

buy	kaufen	
at MARTINS	bei MARTINS	
for	für	
pound (£)	Pfund *(britische Währung)*	! du schreibst: **£5** du sagst: five **pounds**
pencil sharpener	Bleistiftanspitzer	
rubber	Radiergummi	
ruler	Lineal	
give	geben	
pen	Kugelschreiber, Stift; Füller	
pencil	Bleistift	
pencil case	Federmäppchen	
calculator	Taschenrechner	
exercise book	Schulheft, Übungsheft	
weekend	Wochenende	
Saturday	Samstag	
Sunday	Sonntag	
classroom	Klassenraum	
in English	auf Englisch	
speak (to)	sprechen (mit)	
borrow	(aus)leihen, sich borgen	
sure	sicher	
Here you are.	Bitte schön. / Hier, bitte.	
next	nächste(r, s)	
German	Deutsch; deutsch	
start	anfangen	
with	mit	

we aren't	wir sind nicht
you're (= you are)	du bist, ihr seid, Sie sind
student	Schüler/in; Student/in
seventeen	siebzehn →
love	lieben, sehr mögen

15 fifteen	19 nineteen	...
16 sixteen	20 twenty	30 thirty
17 seventeen	21 twenty-one	31 thirty-one
18 eighteen	22 twenty-two	...

Unit 2: At home with Ellie

house	Haus
flat	Wohnung
kitchen	Küche
room	Raum, Zimmer
in the photo	auf dem Foto
nice	nett, schön
bedroom	Schlafzimmer
garden	Garten
living room	Wohnzimmer
toilet	Toilette
bathroom	Bad(ezimmer)
mum	Mama, Mutti
live	leben, wohnen
her dad	ihr Vater →

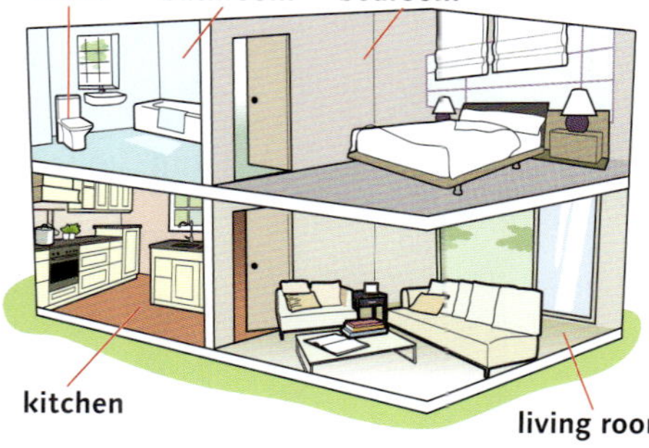

my	mein/e	**his**	sein/e
your	dein/e, euer/eure	**her**	ihr/e

Theme 1

family	Familie
upstairs	oben; nach oben
stepdad	Stiefvater
stepmum	Stiefmutter
miss	vermissen
his partner	sein Partner, seine Partnerin
cute	niedlich, süß
you're lucky	du hast Glück
family tree	(Familien-) Stammbaum
grandpa	Opa
grandma	Oma
stepsister	Stiefschwester

stepbrother	Stiefbruder	

Theme 2

problem	Problem	
happy	glücklich, froh	
unhappy	unglücklich	🙂 **happy ◂▸ unhappy** 🙁
look at	anschauen	
shoe	Schuh	
messy	unordentlich	
too small	zu klein	**small ◂▸ big**
table	Tisch	
I do my homework.	ich mache (meine) Hausaufgaben.	! *Englisch:* **Homework is** important. *Deutsch:* **Hausaufgaben sind** wichtig.
place	Ort, Platz, Stelle	
noisy	laut, voller Lärm	
lamp	Lampe	
chair	Stuhl	
bed	Bett	
again	wieder, noch einmal	
tomorrow	morgen	
to	zu, nach, in	
after school	nach der Schule	**after ◂▸ before**
at the cinema	im Kino	
me	mir; mich	
in town	in der Stadt	

Focus on language

tired	müde	
very happy	sehr glücklich	
at a restaurant	in einem Restaurant	
It's her birthday.	Sie hat Geburtstag.	
really	wirklich	Our English teacher is **really** nice.
text (message)	SMS	
a text **from** mum	eine SMS von Mama	
week	Woche	
write about	schreiben über	
answer	Antwort	
work	arbeiten	

listen (to)	zuhören; (sich etwas) anhören	
picture	Bild	
banana	Banane	
address	Adresse	What's your address? 11 Greatfield Street.
phone number	Telefonnummer	
talk about	sprechen über	
surprise	Überraschung	
often	oft	
all	alle(s)	
Don't be silly.	Sei nicht albern/ dumm/blöd.	
book	Buch	

Unit 3: My Plymouth

sometimes	manchmal	
ride a bike	Rad fahren	

Theme 1

in the morning / afternoon / evening	am Morgen / Nachmittag / Abend	
vegetables	Gemüse	**!** *Englisch*: **Vegetables are** good for you. *Deutsch*: **Gemüse ist** gut für dich.
always	immer	
meet	kennenlernen; (sich) treffen	
present	Geschenk	
trainer	Sportschuh	
expensive	teuer	The **trainers** are too **expensive**.
then	dann	
terrible	schrecklich	
shirt	Hemd	
stay	bleiben	Can't we **stay** at home?

Theme 2

have a party	eine Party feiern	
parents	Eltern	
September	September	
February	Februar	
August	August	

December	Dezember	
January	Januar	
March	März	
April	April	
May	Mai	
June	Juni	
July	Juli	
October	Oktober	
November	November	**1st first** 1. **2nd second** 2. **3rd third** 3. **4th fourth** 4.
second	zweite(r, s) →	
when?	wann?	
Happy birthday!	Herzlichen Glückwunsch zum Geburtstag!	! *Englisch*: When **is your birthday**? *Deutsch*: Wann **hast du Geburtstag**?
do	machen, tun	
something	etwas	
Shut up!	Halt den Mund!	! Vorsicht: **Shut up!** klingt sehr unhöflich.
there	da, dort; dahin, dorthin	
at work	bei der Arbeit, am Arbeitsplatz	
first	zuerst	
leg	Bein	
fall	fallen; hinfallen	
back from the hospital	aus dem Krankenhaus zurück	
want	wollen	! I **want** a new bike. Ich **möchte** ein neues Fahrrad (haben). **I want to buy it now.** Ich **möchte** es jetzt kaufen.
end	Ende, Schluss	
come	(mit)kommen	
price	(Kauf-)Preis	
garage sale	Garagenflohmarkt *(privater Flohmarkt)*	
get	bekommen, kriegen	I always **get** nice presents on my birthday.
money	Geld	
fifty	fünfzig	
question	Frage	
ask	fragen	**ask ◂▸ answer**
play	spielen	

Sounds fun.	Hört sich gut an. / Klingt, als ob es Spaβ macht.	
at one o'clock	um 1 Uhr / um 13 Uhr	It's **1 o'clock** now. 
home	nach Hause	

Focus on language

get up	aufstehen	
early	früh	
go by bus	mit dem Bus fahren	I often **go** to school **by bus**. My brother always **goes by bike**.
walk	(zu Fuβ) gehen, wandern	
make	machen, herstellen	
breakfast	Frühstück	
dinner	Abendessen	

Unit 4: Berry's world

lots of …	viel …, viele …	
visitor	Besucher/in, Gast	
watch	*sich etwas* anschauen; beobachten	
child, *pl* **children**	Kind, Kinder	
ride a pony	auf einem Pony/ ein Pony reiten	You can **ride** a bike or **ride** a pony. 
pet	Haustier	
everybody	jeder; alle	
on	auf	! *Englisch*: **on** the farm — **on** Monday *Deutsch*: **auf** dem Bauernhof — **am** Montag
cow	Kuh	
pig	Schwein	
sheep, *pl* **sheep**	Schaf, Schafe	 ! one **sheep** two **sheep** 
chicken	Huhn; (Brat-) Hähnchen	

Theme 1

from Monday **to** Friday	von Montag bis Freitag	
wake	wecken	
other	andere(r, s)	

outside	draußen; nach draußen	
feed	füttern	
look after	sich kümmern um; aufpassen auf	
What's the time?	Wie spät ist es?	
clock	Uhr	
You're welcome.	Bitte, gern geschehen. / Nichts zu danken.	

Theme 2

when	wenn	**!** **1. wann:** **When** is your birthday? **2. wenn:** I feel good **when** I do sport.
feel fed up	genervt sein, sauer sein; die Nase voll haben	
work	funktionieren	
text me	mir eine SMS schicken	
my bus **is late**	mein Bus hat Verspätung	
because	weil	I feel fed up **because** my bus is late.
the only student	der einzige Schüler / die einzige Schülerin	
wheelchair	Rollstuhl	
can't (= cannot)	nicht können	
at night	nachts, in der Nacht	
Let's … (= let us)	Lass uns … / Lasst uns …	
to the country	aufs Land	
there's … / there are …	es ist … / es gibt … es sind … / es gibt …	**There's** a ruler, but **there are** no pencils.
excited	aufgeregt, gespannt	

a **wheelchair**

Focus on language

shoulder	Schulter	
wet	nass	
laugh	lachen	**!** du schreibst **laugh** – du sprichst ein langes **a**
eat	essen; fressen	

Story

through	durch	**!** du schreibst **through** - du sprichst ein langes **u**
field	Feld; Weide	
dangerous	gefährlich	
noise	Geräusch; Lärm	
only	nur, bloß	
city	(Groß-)Stadt	
hear	hören	

Skills training

sign	Schild; Zeichen
get the bus	den Bus nehmen
left	links; nach links
bring	bringen, mitbringen

5 pm	5 Uhr nachmittags / abends / 17 Uhr
5 am	5 Uhr morgens / vormittags
Dear …	Liebe … / Lieber …
hope	hoffen
thank you	danke (schön)
Best wishes	Viele Grüße, … *(Briefschluss)*
date	Datum
funny	lustig
use	benutzen

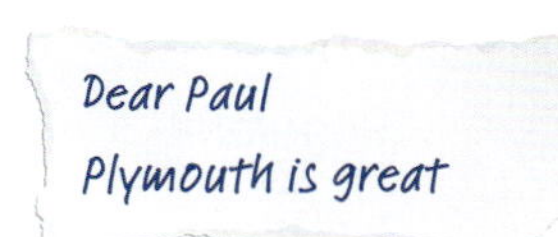

Unit 5: All about Adam

Theme 1

customer	Kunde, Kundin
chips *(pl)*	Pommes frites
soup	Suppe
cream	Sahne
salad	Salat *(als Gericht oder Beilage)*
tea	Tee

coffee	Kaffee
juice	Saft
water	Wasser
cook	kochen
never	nie, niemals →
wash up	abwaschen
of course	natürlich, selbstverständlich

never	**sometimes**	**often**	**always**
nie	manchmal	oft	immer

him	ihn; ihm
hard	schwer; schwierig; hart
must	müssen
letter	Brief
phone	anrufen
need	brauchen
today	heute
trouble	Ärger, Schwierigkeit(en)

Theme 2

so boring	so langweilig	
I'll phone (= I will phone) …	ich werde … anrufen	
about	ungefähr	
why?	warum?	
send	schicken, senden	
guitar	Gitarre	! *Englisch*: I play **the guitar** / **the piano**. *Deutsch*: Ich spiele **Gitarre** / **Klavier**.
piano	Klavier	
sing	singen	

Story

make a difference	etwas bewirken, etwas ausmachen	
it **was** Friday	es war Freitag	
some	einige, ein paar; etwas	
they **were** on the bus	sie waren im Bus	
face	Gesicht	
he **said**	er sagte; er hat gesagt	
nothing	nichts	
angry	wütend, ärgerlich	
life, *pl* **lives**	*(das)* Leben, *(die)* Leben	! one **life** – nine **lives**

for example	zum Beispiel
proud (of)	stolz (auf)

Focus on language

food	Essen, Lebensmittel; Futter
drink	Getränk
cheese	Käse
jam	Marmelade
Anything else?	Sonst noch etwas?
a **bottle (of …)**	eine Flasche …
soon	bald

two bottles of juice

a **bottle of water**

Skills training

under	unter →
in front of	vor →
bag	Tasche
behind	hinter →
next to	neben →
on the left	links, auf der linken Seite
in the middle	in der Mitte
on the right	rechts, auf der rechten Seite
man, *pl* **men**	Mann, Männer
woman, *pl* **women**	Frau, Frauen
difficult	schwierig

The hamster is …

behind the TV

in front of the TV

on the TV

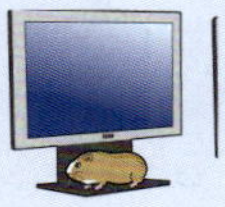

under the TV

next to the TV

English numbers

0 oh, zero, nil	11 eleven	30 thirty	1st first
1 one	12 twelve	40 forty	2nd second
2 two	13 thirteen	50 fifty	3rd third
3 three	14 fourteen	60 sixty	4th fourth
4 four	15 fifteen	70 seventy	5th fifth
5 five	16 sixteen	80 eighty	6th sixth
6 six	17 seventeen	90 ninety	7th seventh
7 seven	18 eighteen	100 a/one hundred	8th eighth
8 eight	19 nineteen	…	9th ninth
9 nine	20 twenty		10th tenth
10 ten	21 twenty-one		…
	22 twenty-two		
	23 twenty-three		
	…		

A

a ein/e
about
1. ungefähr
2. über
• **talk about** sprechen über
• **What about you?** Und du? / Was ist mit dir? • **write about** schreiben über
address Adresse
after school nach der Schule
afternoon Nachmittag
again wieder; noch einmal
all alle(s)
always immer
am **I'm (= I am)** ich bin
am **5 am** 5 Uhr morgens/vormittags
an ein/e *(vor Vokalen)*
and und
angry wütend, ärgerlich
animal Tier
answer Antwort
Anything else? Sonst noch etwas?
April April
are
1. bist; seid
2. sind
aren't **(are not)** bist nicht; seid nicht; sind nicht
art Kunst
ask fragen
at **at MARTINS** bei MARTINS
• **at a restaurant** in einem Restaurant • **at home** zu Hause
• **at school** in der Schule
• **at the cinema** im Kino
August August
away weg, fort

B

babysitter Babysitter
back zurück
bad schlecht; schlimm
bag Tasche
banana Banane
basketball Basketball
bathroom Badezimmer
be sein
beach Strand
because weil
bed Bett
bedroom Schlafzimmer
before bevor; vor
behind hinter
best beste(r, s); am besten
• **Best wishes** Viele Grüße, … *(Briefschluss)*
big groß
bike Fahrrad
bird Vogel
birthday Geburtstag • **Happy birthday!** Herzlichen Glückwunsch zum Geburtstag! • **It's her birthday.** Sie hat Geburtstag.
black schwarz
blue blau
boat Boot; Schiff
book Buch
boring langweilig
borrow (aus)leihen, sich borgen
bottle Flasche
box Box, Kasten
boy Junge
break Pause
breakfast Frühstück
bring bringen, mitbringen
brother Bruder
brown braun
bus Bus
but aber
buy kaufen
by bus/bike/car mit dem Bus/Rad/Auto • **go by bus** mit dem Bus fahren
Bye. Tschüs.

C

calculator Taschenrechner
can können
can't **(= cannot)** nicht können
car Auto
cat Katze
CD CD
chair Stuhl
cheese Käse
chicken Huhn; (Brat-)Hähnchen
child, *pl* **children** Kind, Kinder
chips *(pl)* Pommes frites
cinema Kino
city (Groß-)Stadt
class (Schul-)Klasse
class teacher Klassenlehrer/in
classroom Klassenraum
clock Uhr
coffee Kaffee
colour Farbe
come (mit)kommen
computer Computer
cook kochen
cool cool
country Land
cow Kuh
crab Krebs
cream Sahne
customer Kunde, Kundin
cute niedlich, süß

D

dad Papa, Vati
dancing *(das)* Tanzen
dangerous gefährlich
date Datum
day Tag
Dear … Liebe … / Lieber …
December Dezember
difference Unterschied • **make a difference** etwas bewirken, etwas ausmachen
different unterschiedlich, verschieden, anders
difficult schwierig
dinner Abendessen
do machen, tun • **I do my homework** ich mache (meine) Hausaufgaben
dog Hund
drink Getränk
DVD DVD

E

early früh
eat essen; fressen
eight acht
elephant Elefant
eleven elf
else: **Anything else?** Sonst noch etwas?
email E-Mail
end Ende, Schluss
England England
English Englisch; englisch
evening Abend
everybody jeder; alle
example Beispiel
• **for example** zum Beispiel
excited aufgeregt, gespannt

exercise book Schulheft, Übungsheft
expensive teuer

F

face Gesicht
fall fallen; hinfallen
family Familie • **family tree** (Familien-)Stammbaum
farm Bauernhof
favourite Lieblings- • **favourite thing** Lieblingssache
February Februar
fed up: feel fed up genervt sein, sauer sein; die Nase voll haben
feed füttern
feel sich fühlen; fühlen
field Feld; Weide
fifty fünfzig
film Film
fine gut, schön • **I'm fine.** Es geht mir gut.
firefighter Feuerwehrmann, Feuerwehrfrau
first zuerst • **first (= 1st)** erste, erster, erstes
five fünf
flat Wohnung
food Essen, Lebensmittel; Futter
football Fußball
for für
four vier
fourteen vierzehn
Friday Freitag
friend Freund/in
from
1. aus • **I'm from Plymouth.** Ich bin/komme aus Plymouth.
2. von • **from Monday to Friday** von Montag bis Freitag • **a text from mum** eine SMS von Mama
front: in front of vor
funny lustig

G

game Spiel
garage Garage • **garage sale** Garagenflohmarkt *(privater Flohmarkt)*
garden Garten
German Deutsch; deutsch
Germany Deutschland
get bekommen, kriegen • **get the bus** den Bus nehmen • **get up** aufstehen
girl Mädchen
give geben
go gehen; fahren • **go away** weggehen
good gut • **Good morning.** Guten Morgen. • **Have a good day.** Ich wünsche dir einen schönen Tag. / Schönen Tag noch.
Goodbye. Auf Wiedersehen.
grandma Oma
grandpa Opa
great großartig, toll
green grün
guitar Gitarre

H

happy glücklich, froh • **Happy birthday!** Herzlichen Glückwunsch zum Geburtstag!
hard schwer, schwierig; hart
has hat
have haben • **Have a good day.** Ich wünsche dir einen schönen Tag. / Schönen Tag noch
he **he's (= he is)** er ist
hear hören
Hello. Hallo
help Hilfe
her sie, ihr **her dad** ihr Vater
here hier; hierher • **Here you are.** Bitte schön. / Hier, bitte.
Hi! Hallo.
him ihn; ihm
hip hop Hip-Hop
his his partner sein Partner, seine Partnerin
hobby Hobby
holidays Ferien
home nach Hause • **at home** zu Hause
homework Hausaufgabe/n
hope hoffen
hospital Krankenhaus
house Haus
how wie • **How are you?** Wie geht's? / Wie geht es dir/euch?
hundred • **a hundred, one hundred** (ein)hundert

I

I ich • **I'm (= I am)** ich bin
idea Idee
I'll ich werde
important wichtig
in in • **in English** auf Englisch • **in the morning/afternoon/evening** am Morgen/Nachmittag/Abend
interview Interview
is ist • **he/she/it isn't (= is not)** er/sie/es ist nicht
it es, (*bei Dingen und Tieren*) er, sie • **it's (= it is)** es ist (*bei Dingen und Tieren auch:* er ist, sie ist)

J

jam Marmelade
January Januar
jeans Jeans
juice Saft
July Juli
June Juni

K

kid Kind, Jugendliche/r
kitchen Küche
know wissen; kennen

L

lamp Lampe
laptop Laptop
last letzte(r, s)
late (zu) spät • **my bus is late** mein Bus hat Verspätung
laugh lachen
left links; nach links • **on the left** links, auf der linken Seite
leg Bein
lesson (Unterrichts-)Stunde
let's (= let us) lass(t) uns
letter Brief
life, *pl* **lives** *(das)* Leben, *(die)* Leben
like mögen • **I don't like …** ich mag … nicht
listen zuhören • **listen to** (sich etwas) anhören
live leben, wohnen • **she lives** sie lebt/wohnt
living room Wohnzimmer
look sehen, schauen • **look after** sich kümmern um; aufpassen auf • **look at** anschauen

lots of viel(e)
love lieben, sehr mögen
lucky • **you're lucky** du hast Glück
lunch Mittagessen

M

make machen, herstellen
man, *pl* **men** Mann, Männer
March März
maths Mathematik
May Mai
me mir; mich • **It's me.** Ich bin's.
meet kennenlernen; (sich) treffen
men (➜ man) Männer
messy unordentlich
middle Mitte • **in the middle** in der Mitte
miss vermissen
mobile (phone) Handy
Monday Montag
money Geld
morning Morgen • **Good morning.** Guten Morgen.
Mr Smith Herr Smith
Mrs Smith Frau Smith
mum Mama, Mutti
music Musik
must müssen
my mein/e

N

name Name • **What's your name?** Wie heißt du?
need brauchen
never nie, niemals
new neu
next nächste(r, s) • **next to** neben
nice nett, schön
night Nacht • **at night** nachts, in der Nacht
nine neun
no kein/e
no nein
noise Geräusch; Lärm
noisy laut, voller Lärm
not nicht; kein/e
nothing nichts
November November
now nun, jetzt
number Nummer

O

o'clock: at one o'clock um 1 Uhr / um 13 Uhr
October Oktober
of von • **the last day of the holidays** der letzte Tag der Ferien
of course natürlich, selbstverständlich
often oft
OK okay, gut • **I'm OK.** Es geht mir gut.
old alt
on auf • **on Monday** am Montag
one eins
only nur, bloß • **the only student** der einzige Schüler / die einzige Schülerin
or oder
orange orange
other andere(r, s)
our unser/e
outside draußen; nach draußen

P

parents Eltern
park Park
partner Partner/in
party Party • **have a party** eine Party feiern
PE (physical education) (Schul-)Sport
pen Kugelschreiber, Stift; Füller
pencil Bleistift
pencil case Federmäppchen
pencil sharpener Bleistiftanspitzer
people Leute, Menschen
pet Haustier
phone
1. anrufen
2. Telefon
phone number Telefonnummer
photo Foto
piano Klavier
picture Bild
pig Schwein
pink rosa
place Ort, Platz, Stelle
play spielen • **playing games** Spiele spielen
please bitte
pm 5 pm 5 Uhr nachmittags/abends/17 Uhr
poster Poster
pound (£) Pfund *(britische Währung)*
present Geschenk
price (Kauf-)Preis
principal Schulleiter/in
problem Problem
proud (of) stolz (auf)

Q

question Frage
quiz Quiz

R

rap Rap
read lesen • **reading** *(das)* Lesen
really nice wirklich nett
red rot
remember daran denken, nicht vergessen; sich erinnern an
restaurant Restaurant
ride
1. reiten • **ride a pony** auf einem Pony/ein Pony reiten
2. fahren • **ride a bike** Rad fahren
right richtig • **that's right** das stimmt, das ist richtig
right rechts • **on the right** rechts, auf der rechten Seite
rock (music) Rock(musik)
room Raum, Zimmer
rubber Radiergummi
ruler Lineal

S

said (➜ say) he said er sagte; er hat gesagt
salad Salat *(als Gericht oder Beilage)*
sale Verkauf; Schlussverkauf
sandwich Sandwich
Saturday Samstag
say sagen • **Ellie says** Ellie sagt • **he said** er sagte; er hat gesagt
school Schule
second zweite(r, s)
see sehen • **See you.** Bis dann./Tschüs.

send schicken, senden
September September
seven sieben
seventeen siebzehn
sharpener Anspitzer
she sie *(weibliche Person)* • **she's (= she is)** sie ist
sheep, *pl* **sheep** Schaf, Schafe
shirt Hemd
shoe Schuh
shoulder Schulter
show Show, Vorführung, Aufführung
Shut up! Halt den Mund!
sign Schild; Zeichen
silly albern, dumm, blöd
sing singen
sister Schwester
six sechs
small klein
snack Snack, kleine Mahlzeit
so boring so langweilig
some einige, ein paar; etwas
something etwas
sometimes manchmal
soon bald
Sorry. / I'm sorry. Tut mir leid. / Entschuldigung.
sound klingen, sich anhören • **Sounds fun.** Hört sich gut an. / Klingt, als ob es Spaß macht.
soup Suppe
speak sprechen • **speak (to)** sprechen (mit) • **speaking to friends** mit Freunden/Freundinnen sprechen
start anfangen • **it starts** er/sie/es fängt an
stay bleiben
stepbrother Stiefbruder
stepdad Stiefvater
stepmum Stiefmutter
stepsister Stiefschwester
student Schüler/in; Student/in
stupid dumm, blöd; albern
summer Sommer
Sunday Sonntag
sure sicher
surprise Überraschung
sweets Bonbons, Süßigkeiten
swim schwimmen • **swimming** *(das)* Schwimmen • **go swimming** schwimmen gehen

T

table Tisch
talk sprechen • **talk about** sprechen über
tea Tee
teacher Lehrer/in
teenager Teenager
ten zehn
terrible schrecklich
text eine SMS schicken • **text (message)** SMS
thank you danke (schön)
thanks danke
the der, die, das
then dann
there da, dort; dahin, dorthin • **there are …** es sind … / es gibt … • **there's** es ist … / es gibt …
they sie *(Mehrzahl)* • **they're (= they are)** sie sind
thing Ding, Sache
think denken, meinen, glauben
third dritte(r, s)
thirteen dreizehn
this diese(r, s) • **This is …** Dies ist … / Das ist …
three drei
through durch
Thursday Donnerstag
tie Krawatte
time Zeit; Uhrzeit • **What's the time?** Wie spät ist es?
timetable Stundenplan
tired müde
to zu, nach, in • **to the country** aufs Land • **from Monday to Friday** von Montag bis Freitag • **go to dad's flat** in Papas Wohnung gehen
today heute
toilet Toilette
tomorrow morgen
too auch
too small zu klein
town Stadt • **in town** in der Stadt
trainer Sportschuh
tree Baum
trouble Ärger, Schwierigkeit(en)
T-shirt T-Shirt
Tuesday Dienstag
TV Fernseher
twelve zwölf
two zwei

U

under unter
unhappy unglücklich
unit Unit • **unit quiz** Unit-Quiz
upstairs oben; nach oben
us uns
use benutzen

V

vegetables Gemüse
very sehr
visitor Besucher/in, Gast

W

wake wecken
walk (zu Fuß) gehen, wandern
want wollen • **want to buy** kaufen wollen
was war
wash up abwaschen
watch *sich etwas* anschauen; beobachten • **watching TV** Fernsehen
water Wasser
we wir • **we're (= we are)** wir sind
Wednesday Mittwoch
week Woche
weekday Werktag, Wochentag
weekend Wochenende
welcome: Welcome to Plymouth. Willkommen in Plymouth! • **You're welcome.** Bitte, gern geschehen. / Nichts zu danken.
were waren
wet nass
what
1. was
2. welche(r, s)
• **What about you?** Und du? / Was ist mit dir? • **What's your name?** Wie heißt du? • **What's …? (= What is …?)** Was ist …?
wheelchair Rollstuhl
when
1. wann
2. wenn

• **When's (= when is) your birthday?** Wann hast du Geburtstag?
where wo(hin)
white weiß
who wer • **Who are you?** Wer bist du? / Wer seid ihr?
why? warum?
will werden • **I'll phone (= I will phone) ...** ich werde ... anrufen
wish: Best wishes Viele Grüße, ... *(Briefschluss)*
with mit
woman, *pl* **women** Frau, Frauen
work
1. arbeiten
2. funktionieren
• **at work** bei der Arbeit, am Arbeitsplatz
write schreiben
wrong falsch • **that's wrong** das stimmt nicht, das ist falsch

Y

yellow gelb
yes ja
you
1. dich; dir; euch; Sie; Ihnen
2. du; ihr; Sie • **you're (= you are)** du bist, ihr seid, Sie sind
your dein/e, euer/eure

QUELLEN

Titelbild
Trevor Burrows Photography, Plymouth

Illustrationen
Stephen Elford, Lemonade Illustration Agency, London, UK (S. 20 oben; S. 22 oben; S. 24; S. 27; S. 28 man; S. 32; S. 34 (u. 38 u. 41 u. 48); S. 35; S. 41 unten li. u. re.; S. 43; S. 55 oben; S. 58; S. 60); **Kate Davies**, Colerne, UK (S. 3; S. 5 sweets; S. 10; S. 14; S. 15; S. 16; S. 17 oben Nr. 1; S. 19; S. 21 unten; S. 22 unten; S. 28 elephants, dog, cat; S. 31; S. 39; S. 45; S. 46; S. 48 oben; S. 49; S. 51; S. 56; S. 57 oben); **Eva Muszyinski**, Berlin (S. 5 oben; S. 9); **David Norman**, Meerbusch (S. 40); **Jeongsook Lee**, Heidelberg (S. 61; S. 62; S. 64; S. 67; S. 68; S. 71; S. 72; S. 73; S. 74); **Tom Percival, Advocate Art**, London, UK (S. 5 unten li. u. re.; S. 7; S. 17 Mitte Nr. 2; S. 18; S. 23; S. 25 Nr. 17 1. Reihe 2. v. li. u. 3. v. li., 2. Reihe 1. v. li., 2. v. li.; S. 52 Mitte, unten; S. 55 unten; S. 57 unten); **Simon Rumble, Beehive Illustration**, Cirencester, UK (S. 6 puzzle; S. 11 PE, history, maths, IT, science, art; S. 20 unten; S. 21 oben; S. 25 Nr. 17 1. Reihe 1. v. li., 2. Reihe 3. v. li.; S. 37 (u. 41 u. 48); S. 53); **Elwood H. Smith**, Rhinebeck, U.S.A. (S. 28 crab); **Dorina Tessmann**, Berlin (S. 6 oben); **Steffen Wolff**, Brohl-Lützing (S. 52 Bild 1-4; S. 66)

Bildquellen
Trevor Burrows Photography, Plymouth (S. 10; S. 13 Bild A, Bild B, Bild D, Bild E; S. 14; S. 16; S. 26 unten; S. 29 Bild 2, unten re.; S. 30 oben, unten; S. 33; S. 40; S. 41; S. 50 Adam holding tea pot); **Cornelsen Schulverlage** (S. 13 Bild C: Britta Bensmann; S. 23: Anja Zieschang; S. 29 swimming pool: Britta Bensmann; S. 35 Bild 1-4: Eva Baumgart/coins used by permission of The British Royal Mint, banknote used by permission of Bank of England); **Corbis**, Düsseldorf (S. 3 oben: Uwe Umstätter/Radius Images); **Fotolia** (S. 39 Bild 4 (u. 47): Tralesta; S. 60 oben li.: goodluz, oben re.: daboost, Mitte li.: Mariusz Blach, Mitte re.: wajan, unten li. u. re.: Syda Productions/lev dolgachov; S. 71: Les Cunliffe); **mauritius images**, Mittenwald (S. 29 Bild 1: way out west photography/Alamy); **Thomas Schulz**, Teupitz (S. 64); **Shutterstock** (S. 3 unten li. (u. 5): Monkey Business Images, unten re. (u. 5): Monkey Business Images; S. 4 girl li.: ZouZou, re.: Gelpi JM, numbers one, two, three, four, five, six: HitToon.Com; S. 5 Bild 3: Monkey Business Images; S. 6 Bild 1: sisqopote, Bild 2: Vasiliy Koval, Bild 3: Eric Issellee, Bild 4: Four Oaks; S. 7 Bild A: Sabphoto, Bild B: Jorg Hackemann, Bild C: Keselev Andrey Valerevich, Bild D: BestPhotoStudio, Bild E: Elena Elisseeva, unten re.: PRIMA; S. 9 Bild 1 u. 4: Gelpi JM, Bild 2: Michael Shake, Bild 3: Blend Images, Bild 5: steamroller_blues, Bild 6: saginbay; S. 11 music: zphoto, German flag u. English flag: JanPetrskovky; S. 12: Spotmatik Ltd; S. 13 Bild F: design36; S. 18 oben li.: Semmick Photo, oben re.: Petar Paunchev, unten li.: Anton Poznyak, unten re.: Thai Soriano; S. 19 Bild 1: photobankch, Bild 2 (u. 37): Dirk Ott, Bild 3 (u. 37): WDG Photo, Bild 4 (u. 37): Sternstunden, Bild 5 (u. 26 u. 27 u. 37): olmarmar, Bild 6 (u. 37): Iriana Shiyan, Bild 7 (u. 37): MR. INTERIOR, Bild 8 (u. 27 u. 37): Iriana Shiyan; S. 25 Bild 1 u. 2 phones (M): pixachi; S. 26 Bild 1: Radu Razvan; Bild 2: Route66, Bild 3: Marques, Bild 4: grzym; S. 27 Bild 1 (u. 35): lynnette, Bild 2: Oleg Elena Tovkach, Bild 3: fotocraft, Bild 4: Elnur, Bild 7: Phiseksit; S. 29 Bild 4: vhpfoto, Bild 5: skyfish, Bild 6: mihas; S. 30 tie: Karina Bakalyan, sweets: Aaron Amat, shirt: Karina Bakalyan, jeans: nito, trainers: ericlefrancais; S. 32 Bild 1: Konstantin Chagin, Bild 2: cristovao, Bild 3: Accord, Bild 4: Apollofoto, Bild 5: Monkey Business Images, Bild 6: Max Topchii; S. 34 oben: kaarsten, unten li. u. re.: SergiyN; S. 35 two chairs: photka, lamp: DuleS, Bild 1: Coprid, Bild 2: Julia Ivantsova, Bild 3: Pakhnyushchy, Bild 4: Julia Ivantsova; S. 36 Bild A: plane: Bannykh Alexey Vladimirovich, palm: sabri deniz kizil, Bild B: Spinsugar; S. 39 Bild 1: David Hughes, Bild 2 (u. 47): Dariusz Gora, Bild 3 (u. 47): lyly, Bild 5: Pressmaster, Bild 6: MARCELODLT; S. 42: Galina Barskaya; S. 45: Vlad61; S. 46: James Steidl; S. 47 Bild 2: Irina Bondareva, Bild 4: robertoserratore, Bild 5: Eastimages, Bild 6: Thomas Skjaeveland; S. 50 oben Bild 1: Aaron Amat, oben Bild 2: MaraZe, oben Bild 3: Meleena, oben Bild 4: Preto Perola, oben Bild 5: Marko Bradic, oben Bild 6: Maria_OH, oben Bild 7: Evgeny Karandaev, oben Bild 8: Evgeny Karandaev, unten Bild 1: Peter Gudella, Bild 2: RTimages, Bild 3: Dmitry Kalinovsky, Bild 4: snai aksoy, Bild 5: fotostoker, Bild 6: MilousSK; S. 51 Bild 1: Roman Seliutin, Bild 2: ZouZou, Bild 3: Pixachi, Bild 4: Pefkos; S. 55 glass of orange juice (M): DenisNata, banana (M): Tischenko Irina, sandwich: Christopher Elwell, orange: Tim UR; S. 58 oben li. two teenagers: Orange Line Media, Bild 1: Sean Locke Photography, Bild 2: Andrey_Popov, Bild 3: Aleksandr Markin, Bild 4: mzsy; S. 72 oben: Gemenacom, unten: Vereshchagin Dmitry; S. 75 juice: Nito, water: R. Gino Santa Maria, numbers: HitToon.Com)